Endorsements

To   nds are the joy of life and in writing about networking as he has
Ste   ouza has gone right to the heart of the matter – anything that
car   age us to exchange ideas and learn from each other must be a
goo   g.

Carole Stone, Managing Director of YouGovStone Ltd

Con   g is essential to networking and networking is vital to creating
more   ections. This book is an essential guide for both personal and
caree   cess.

Patrick Clarke, Director of Connections, EDF Energy

You r   t meet a partner for life or business or just share ideas,
expe   ces and build something new from the simple effort of
intro   ng yourself. After reading *Brilliant networking* you'll want to
say 'Y   to any invite.

John Bird CBE, Founder of the Big Issue

Brillia   networking is an important reminder that relationship building is
at the   eart of personal and professional success. In easy and clear steps it
demo   strates the ingredients to network effectively.

Preethi Nair, Bestselling author and playwright

With   rapidly changing economy affecting the way we do business,
netw   king remains the most effective way for most business people to
thriv   Helping us find sales, support, confidence and knowledge, *Brilliant
netw   ing* skills are vital for both individual and company success.

dy Lopata, Business Networking Strategist, co-author of And Death
C   e Third! The Definitive Guide to Networking and Speaking in Public

I learn quite late in my career that your personal and professional
networks open doors, facilitate business development and support you in
navigating the sometimes complex world of work. *Brilliant networking* is
a welcome resource.

*Fleur Bothwick, Head of Diversity and Inclusiveness,
Ernst & Young LLP*

Brilliant networking is a vital tool to master. Steven D'Souza helps you to understand and practise this very important aspect of business success in a fashion that is both easy to understand and simple to follow.

Pinky Lilani OBE, Chairman, Asian Women of Achievement Awards, Women of the Future Awards and Inspirational Women's Network

Much of the fear we have of connecting with new people is will they like me or reject me? I always think what's the worst that can happen? *Brilliant networking* is a great book of tips that will make any approach from you irresistible!

Sandra Kerr, National Director, Race for Opportunity, Business in the Community

Treasuring friendships and relationships is crucial to success and happiness in every area of life. Steven teaches you how to build networks in ways that are easy and natural to you.

Nick Williams, author of The Work We Were Born To Do **(www.nick-williams.com)**

In today's co-creation orientated world, *Brilliant networking* reminds each one of us that the human interactions we choose and cultivate embody our unique contribution to value creation.

Joseph Pistrui, Ph.D, Associate Dean, Executive Education, IE Business School

Relationships are built on trust, integrity and results. *Brilliant networking* is an essential guide to creating these lasting relationships for both personal and professional success.

Eva Castillo, MD, Former Head of Bank of America, Merrill Lynch Wealth Management EMEA

Networking is positive engagement with the world. This brilliant book shows you how to do it naturally and comfortably. Whether you're a novice or expert networker, this book is full of good advice for you.

Wayne Baker, Robert P. Thome Professor of Business Administration, Stephen M. Ross School of Business, University of Michigan

networking

**What the best networkers know,
do and say**

second edition

Steven D'Souza

**Prentice Hall
is an imprint of**

Harlow, England • London • New York • Boston • San Francisco • Toronto • Sydney • Singapore • Hong Kong
Tokyo • Seoul • Taipei • New Delhi • Cape Town • Madrid • Mexico City • Amsterdam • Munich • Paris • Milan

PEARSON EDUCATION LIMITED

Edinburgh Gate
Harlow CM20 2JE
Tel: +44 (0)1279 623623
Fax: +44 (0)1279 431059
Website: www.pearsoned.co.uk

First published in Great Britain in 2008
Second edition 2011

© Pearson Education Limited 2008, 2011

The right of Steven D'Souza to be identified as author of this work has been
asserted by him in accordance with the Copyright, Designs and Patents Act 1988.

ISBN: 978-0-273-74321-7

Pearson Education are not responsible for the content of any third-party
internet sites.

British Library Cataloguing-in-Publication Data
A catalogue record for this book is available from the British Library

Library of Congress Cataloging-in-Publication Data
D'Souza. Steven.
  Brilliant networking : what the best networkers know, do, and say /
Steven D'Souza. -- 2nd ed.
    p. cm.
  Includes bibliographical references and index.
  ISBN 978-0-273-74321-7 (pbk. : alk. paper) 1. Business networks. 2.
Interpersonal relations. 3. Social networks. I. Title.
  HD69.S8D74 2011
  650.1'3--dc22
                          2010041912

ARP Impression 98

Typeset in 10/14 Plantin by 30
Printed in Great Britain by Clays Ltd, St Ives plc

Con

About the author

Steven D'Souza is an experienced international organisational consultant, speaker, writer, coach and educator. He has worked globally in the fields of HR, Leadership and Talent Management, Organisational Development and Executive Education. He is currently an Executive Fellow of IE Business School, Madrid, and Programme Orchestrator of the Global Senior Management Program for Chicago Booth Business School.

Steven is a sought after speaker with many of the leading Fortune 500 and FTSE 100 companies. The first edition of *Brilliant networking* was featured in The *Independent*'s 'Success at Work' series and has been translated into several languages. Steven is also the author of *Made in Britain* which was sponsored for schools to inspire positive role models. He currently lives in London.

Acknowledgements

I firstly want to thank my family, Silo, Christine, Selwyn and Charlene who were my first network and are there for me no matter what. Special thanks go to Bobo West for his contribution to the chapter on technology and networking and to Andy Lopata, David Pearl, David McQueen, Elena Moreno and Katie Ledger all who contributed new material in the last bonus chapter of the second edition of this book.

Thank you also to my friends and colleagues for their encouragement. Especially my team at IE Business School, Joseph Pistrui a brilliant manager and thought partner, and Ulrike Klaussner, Erik Schlie and Alicia Romero my CLG colleagues. Thank you to Sam Jackson, Linda Dhondy and Sarah Wild, and all at Prentice Hall for believing in the potential of this book and working as a team to bring it to you – the reader. Thanks to Marcella Frati for publishing the Italian translation of my book and to Alan Perry my website designer.

Most of all, thank you to all my clients and those in the 'Brilliant networking' community that contributed to the book and who sent their stories, tips and advice to share with you. If you have not been directly mentioned in the text it is an oversight on my part and I appreciate what you have contributed. It genuinely took a network to write this book and I hope the network continues to grow with you, the reader.

Publisher's acknowledgements

We are grateful to the following for permission to reproduce copyright material:

Screenshots on pages 85 and 86 reproduced with permission from Mindjet; Figure on page 227 reprinted from Burt, R. (2005) *Brokerage and Closure: An Introduction to Social Capital*, Figure 1.1, page 14. Reprinted with permission from Oxford University Press; Figure on page 230 adapted from Burt, R. (2005) *Brokerage and Closure: An Introduction to Social Capital*, Figure 1.2, page 21. Reprinted with permission from Oxford University Press; Figures on pages 237 and 239 reprinted from Cross, R. *et al.* (2002) 'Making invisible work visible: using social network analysis to support strategic collaboration', *California Management Review* 44(2): 25–46. Copyright © 2002 by The Regents of the University of California. By permission of The Regents.

Foreword

Lord Bilimoria CBE DL, Founder and Executive Chairman, Cobra Beer

We all know the old saying 'knowledge is power' – but what is too often forgotten is that *who* you know is every bit as important as *what* you know. Contacts and relationships can be crucial, and developing your network is among the most important aspects of business.

When I started Cobra Beer in 1989 I had a business partner, my best friend, but I also had a network of family, friends, business contacts and acquaintances. And what for me is so wonderful about networking – and indeed about the story of Cobra – is how many of these people still work with the company and still support the brand, whether they're employees, suppliers, customers or consumers. This is the essence of networking and the importance of connecting with people: it isn't about having a drawer full of business cards or meeting that one-off contact who can get you something. It's about building strong, long-lasting friendships and relationships.

Networking is also about being proactive. Anyone can sit there and say they're too busy, they're stuck behind their desks – when on earth can I network? – but you've got to make the effort and go out and engage. People talk about the chance meetings that changed their lives – a meeting with a spouse, perhaps, or a business partner – and the simple reality of networking is that the more you do it, the more you increase the chances of those chance meetings. It takes an effort, of course, but there's no substitute for just getting out there, engaging and getting on with it.

And so welcome to *Brilliant networking* by Steven D'Souza. In these pages you'll find everything you need to know about building a great network, including the vital 'inner game' of networking – developing the self-confidence, self-awareness, values and motivation you need even before you start creating contacts. The book also contains insightful tips on using technology and growing your network – a crucial factor in an increasingly globalised and internationally competitive world.

For anyone who wants to meet people, develop contacts and – in business or in life – build those all-important relationships, *Brilliant networking* is, well, brilliant. If you must, keep those old business cards in your drawer. But keep this book on your desk.

Introduction

Welcome to this second edition of *Brilliant networking*. The world has changed dramatically since the first edition, with a global financial crisis, and thousands of job losses worldwide. I believe the principles, ideas and practical tools in this book are now more important than ever, as we re-establish connections and support each other both personally and professionally. Networking is more than just the exchange of business cards. Networking is developing relationships which can support you, and in which you can provide support to others, in every area of life. The wider and stronger our networks, the more capacity and opportunity we have to live life richly and to make life easier for others and ourselves. Networks for great causes and deeper purposes, whether large or small, have the potential to change our world.

Brilliant networkers are rarely born that way. They didn't emerge from the womb being able to do small talk, keep in touch with people and grow their network. Even if they had a feel for networking, they still needed to learn how. And so can you.

Many of the brilliant networkers, whose tips you find in this book, developed their skills through practice – sometimes making many mistakes, collecting lots of rejections but eventually achieving their goals and assisting others to achieve theirs. If you practise the tools and techniques consistently, you will soon come to do them naturally, automatically and comfortably. With patience and practice, there will come a time when you forget you are doing anything consciously and you will just be connecting, and when this happens you will be a brilliant networker.

In this updated second edition you will find a new, bonus, chapter on 'social capital' which describes how the size, structure, quality and diversity of your network can affect your success and can lead to increased pay, faster promotion and better appraisals. The chapter on networking technologies has also been updated to help you take advantage of the rise of Facebook and Twitter.

Finally I have also included a second bonus chapter on networking activities, with fun exercises you can do with your own networks groups.

I hope you enjoy this new edition and it leads to many brilliant connections.

Decide to network!

Steven D'Souza
www.brilliantnetworking.net

Decide to network

Decide to network

Use every letter you write

Every conversation you have

Every meeting you attend

To express your fundamental beliefs and dreams

Affirm to others the vision of the world you want

Network through thought

Network through action

Network through love

Network through spirit

You are the centre of a network

You are the centre of the world

You are a free, immensely powerful source
of life and goodness

Affirm it

Spread it

Radiate it

Think day and night about it

And you will see a miracle happen:
the greatness of your own life

In a world of big powers, media and monopolies

But of [six] and a half billion individuals

Networking is the new freedom
the new democracy
a new form of happiness

Robert Muller, Assistant Secretary General of the United Nations

PART 1

Networking in context

CHAPTER 1

What is networking?

Networking is often one of those things people say you *ought to do* but never quite define exactly what they mean by it. Is networking simply going out to events and conferences or parties and dinner, collecting business cards and trying to make a sale – or is it something far deeper and frankly more rewarding than that? What skills do you actually need to network anyway and is there one type of networking or are there many?

One of the best ways to answer some of the above questions is to introduce you to people you might meet at a so-called 'networking' event. Cast your mind back to the last time you attended an event with people you did not know well and see if you can recognise any of the characters below.

Marketing Martin

'ME ME ME Martin' possesses what psychologists would call a 'marketing personality'. Martin sees others as well as himself as commodities. People are there to be sold to or to buy from. This is no social event for him, it is a sales opportunity.

'What do you do?' Martin asks, as he surveys your sartorial tastes and decides whether or not you are a prospect, hence worth investing time on in conversation. Yet let me not be too harsh on Martin. He does not always talk about himself – that is, he talks about his business plans or his product and tries to 'enrol' you in the benefits and hopefully make a sale!

With a lot of stilted conversation, befuddled metaphors and stories you can't see as quite relevant, you begin to wonder whether Martin has swallowed whole a book on 'how to win friends and manipulate people' or perhaps he went on one of those one-day courses to learn 'people persuasion skills'.

Once Martin has tried at least 101 ways from his sales book to hook you and you know all the benefits of buying 'widgets' from him wholesale, but are still not buying, Martin is gone. He is speaking to the next 'prospect' but not before shoving his business card in your hand and asking you to e-mail any referrals you can think of. Move on Martin!

Talking-at-you Terry

Talking is what Terry does best. After ten minutes you would know everything from what 'status symbols' he owns to how much bonus he took home last year from a deal he clinched like a heroic Sloane ranger. Not many questions, but a lot of answers to questions you never asked would be one of the ways you knew that you were in Terry's company.

The more Terry drones on... and on... the more you want to leave but he seems oblivious. At some points you have something very relevant to say, at least more relevant than Terry's two-bit points, but somehow, no matter how hard you try to edge a word in, Terry's monologue is the only one that is heard.

Eventually another person in the room sees Terry and comes over to join you both, foolishly thinking that you are enjoying a stimulating conversation. You take the opportunity quickly to leave while Terry catches the new victim in his 'talk trap'. You see the same poor fellow there an hour later looking like even a few cans of Red Bull could not wake him from his stupor.

> Terry's monologue is the only one that is heard

Socialite Samantha

Sam is a diva. Everyone spots her as soon as she walks in the room, and before you have the chance to introduce yourself she has the best seat in the room and everybody is talking about her. Pink's 'Let's Get This Party Started' begins to play in the room as all eyes turn to Sam.

Sam drinks only the finest champagne, bought of course by someone else whom she has not met, but is grateful she has come to their event. She pouts like a supermodel while nibbling hand-made truffles delivered by the adoring waiters. She laughs a lot and then seems distant and aloof as though she is in her own 'private universe'.

Only a select few people are around Sam, and she seems to like it that way. She disappears before you even get to 'think' about speaking to her. Off to her next party to 'meet' *more* interesting people who can appreciate her.

Apologetic Andrew

I'm sorry to introduce you to Andrew, but I'm sure if you met him he would more than apologise to you personally. Andrew doesn't seem quite sure how he came to be here tonight as firstly he tells you that he is 'really sorry' that he didn't bring a gift, dress in a way befitting your company, or is not quite simply – interesting.

Andrew apologises for everything. Each time he forgets your name. By the end of the evening you wish that he was a character on a keyboard. If he apologises one more time, 'I swear I'll hit delete!'

Andrew leaves the evening two hours early – after apologising to everyone of course that he needs to get home. But at least he came, not like...

Prefer-to-stay-at-home Peter

You never get to meet this person at an event. Though apparently Peter can be very active and interesting to meet on the internet. Perhaps we'll meet Peter later in the book when we look at networking technology, but – for sure – he's not someone you can have a drink with. OK, maybe a virtual one!

Wallflower Wanda

Peter was impossible to meet but Wanda is just as challenging, even though she is in the room. Wanda looks well dressed, conscientiously so. That's just as well, as any conversation with Wanda is a monologue punctuated with painful long pauses waiting for some reciprocation.

Wanda's positive feature is she is a great listener, but to the extent that her listening could go on for ever, even if there was no one who was talking. And that's the main problem with speaking to Wanda – there is no conversation. Small talk gets a lot smaller, as you seem to have to begin and end every conversation, as well as provide the middle bits.

After a while with Wanda, imagination just takes over where conversation never started. You begin to wonder, 'Maybe she doesn't like me', or 'Perhaps she doesn't get out much'. Due to Wanda's inability to start conversations she sits by herself most of the time and nobody seems to notice.

Kling-on Kevin

You meet Kevin early on in the evening and get on very well. He's someone most people have something in common with, at least in the beginning. You both talk about how you got here, how expensive the drink is and that you have both seen the same film twice at the cinema.

But half an hour later conversation has run a little dry and you both struggle hard to keep going. You look over his shoulder and see a few people that you think would be interesting to meet, but instead Kevin offers to buy you a drink at the bar. Before you know it the evening has passed and you have spent it in banal conversation. But at least the first hour was good. At the end of the evening Kevin scribbles his e-mail on the side of a blue napkin and promises to be in touch in a few weeks to meet up for a drink. In two weeks the napkin is harder to find than a missing person and Kevin might as well have got a role on *Lost* as you never hear from him again!

Connecting Carole

Every evening or event has a highlight and Carole is yours. She approaches you early in the evening, introducing herself, and mentions how you both narrowly escaped being talked at by Terry all evening. Carole has quite a warm personality and seems genuinely interested in you, asking what it was like travelling to Asia in the summer and whether you thought England would ever win the cricket again! She is easy to be with.

One thing that strikes you about Carole is the way she brings people into the conversation almost effortlessly. She seems to know everyone present, as she introduces them by name and can tell you something about them that helps the conversation get started. Later you learn that Carole had just met these people herself.

By the end of the evening everyone has given their contact details to Carole and she has invited them

> you really feel that she genuinely likes you

all to her Christmas Party – a way she has of keeping in contact with people she meets and likes. It's true, you really feel that she genuinely likes you. The day after you met Carole you receive a lovely e-card picture of Singapore with the message 'May your good memories last'. You chuckle and look forward to sending her a newspaper cutting the next time England wins the cricket – which you realise could be quite a while!

So what exactly is networking?

All of the above are of course caricatures of different approaches or ways of being while networking. But it might make you smile if you can recognise any of these characters' qualities, not only in others but also in yourself. But exactly what do we mean by the word 'networking'? Below is a small sample of what a diverse range of people thinks networking is and, more importantly, what they think its purpose is.

Good networking is making the most of the people you meet to your mutual advantage.

Carole Stone, Journalist and Networking Queen

Networking is like a road trip. Working with others to reach a common destination and enjoying the journey.

Martin Berger, PhD student

Networking is using connections with others intelligently.

Simon Jones, Business Analyst

For me, networking is about developing even further your professional reputation and building a support network that you can call upon.

Melvyn De Freitas, Managing Director

Networking is about getting what you want.

Arti Patel, Sales Manager

While these are all different perspectives on the same word, there are common themes:

● Networking is about connections, specifically people connecting. To describe this collection of people I use the word 'community'.

- Networking is not only a support tool but also a resource to help achieve your goals – what you want.
- Networking can enrich your quality of life and the lives of others.
- Networking is a verb. This suggests that it is dynamic in nature. Networks grow but they can also shrink if not maintained.

brilliant definition

Networking is the art of being true to your own values, beliefs and character whilst building and nurturing reciprocal relationships that help individuals or the group as a whole to achieve their goals.

Building a community

One of the key differentiators in this book is that networking is not 'personal'. It's not a 'me, me, me' activity. Brilliant networkers know they are part of a system that operates at a level of reciprocity and that each of us is part of a community intimately involving others.

We are all natural networkers from birth – including you! Networking is something we have all learnt from childhood to get our basic needs met. We may not use the word but everyone in society is in some way involved in a network. The only question is not 'Do we network?' but 'Do we network effectively?'

it's not a 'me, me, me' activity

Brilliant networkers realise that the more diverse reciprocal relationships they have, the more they can benefit from potential options and opportunities.

brilliant tip

Networking is intimately connected to diversity and creativity. The greater the range of options, the greater the possibilities to achieve your goals and assist others.

The communities that networkers build are often not in a fixed location. Perhaps they exhibit diverse interests or are virtual. They might have other communities that flow to and from them, but they are all connected by one common element – the brilliant networker who functions at the hub or is a vital link to each of them.

In the space below write your definition of networking.

Networking is ...

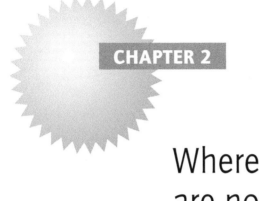

CHAPTER 2

Where you
are now

t's helpful at this point to pause and take a look at how you currently fare as a networker. Once you're aware of your weaker areas you can focus on these and become a brilliant networker in no time at all!

Tick the box that most applies to you:

1. I am very confident in approaching strangers and people I do not know.

   ☐ Never

   ☐ Occasionally

   ☐ Off and on

   ☐ Quite often

   ☐ Always

2. I find it easy to make 'small talk' to keep conversation going.

   ☐ Never

   ☐ Occasionally

   ☐ Off and on

   ☐ Quite often

   ☐ Always

3. I am assertive and confident in asking for what I want from others.

☐ Never

☐ Occasionally

☐ Off and on

☐ Quite often

☐ Always

4. I have an organised system that allows me to search and reach my contacts easily.

☐ Never

☐ Occasionally

☐ Off and on

☐ Quite often

☐ Always

5. I have a wide circle of friends with diverse backgrounds (e.g. age, interests).

☐ Never

☐ Occasionally

☐ Off and on

☐ Quite often

☐ Always

6. I always try to speak to as many people as possible during an event and not just the same person I came with or someone I know well.

☐ Never

☐ Occasionally

☐ Off and on

☐ Quite often

☐ Always

7. I enjoy having new experiences (e.g. going to new places, trying different cuisine).

☐ Never

☐ Occasionally

☐ Off and on

☐ Quite often

☐ Always

8. I feel that I connect deeply and authentically with others and share appropriately about myself.

☐ Never

☐ Occasionally

☐ Off and on

☐ Quite often

☐ Always

9. I remember names and faces, including the small details of the people that I meet.

☐ Never

☐ Occasionally

☐ Off and on

☐ Quite often

☐ Always

10. I find it easy to ask for help when I need it.

☐ Never

☐ Occasionally

☐ Off and on

☐ Quite often

☐ Always

11. I share my contacts freely with others and do all I can to assist when I can.

☐ Never

☐ Occasionally

☐ Off and on

☐ Quite often

☐ Always

12. I am an active member of organisations, clubs and societies that contain thought-leaders in my field of interest.

☐ Never

☐ Occasionally

☐ Off and on

☐ Quite often

☐ Always

13. I take the time to connect regularly with each person in my network, especially when I don't need something. I aim to send useful information or contacts that I think could assist people I know.

☐ Never

☐ Occasionally

☐ Off and on

☐ Quite often

☐ Always

14. I use technology as a tool to help me connect with wider networks.

☐ Never

☐ Occasionally

☐ Off and on

☐ Quite often

☐ Always

Scoring

Total your scores:

- Give yourself 5 for each 'Always' answer.
- Give yourself 4 for each 'Quite often' answer.
- Give yourself 3 for each 'Off and on' answer.
- Give yourself 2 for each 'Occasionally' answer.
- Give yourself 1 for each 'Never' answer.

What your score means

- If you scored between 47 and 70, you are likely to be a strong if not yet a brilliant networker. I hope that this book refines your skills further and you get new ideas.

- If you scored between 23 and 46, you will learn tips in this book to take you to the next level and take you from being an average or good networker to being brilliant.

- If you scored between 14 and 22, you are probably new to networking and this book will give you the ways and means to transform your ability to network successfully. Enjoy!

CHAPTER 3

Why network?

The term 'networking' has received a lot of bad press in the past and many people cringe when the term is used. However, as it is a key tool in helping you to achieve success in your professional and personal life, it's worth quashing these negative myths and firmly establishing why networking is so important that you should embrace all the benefits it can offer.

Six myths of networking

Myth 1: 'Networking is manipulative.'

Networking in this book is fundamentally defined as not a personal but a relationship activity. It means reaching out and connecting to others. Brilliant networkers know that in order to grow their networks they need to develop 'trust'.

Brilliant networkers know trust is built on reciprocity – simply giving and receiving. By being *genuinely attentive* to the needs of others, they build win/win relationships that are the basis of success.

In itself effective networking is a cooperative activity. Manipulation might be effective in the short term but it does not build trust or create lasting and healthy communities in which people want to play an active part.

Myth 2: 'Networking is for socialites who spend all their evenings at cocktail receptions or their weekends sitting through long and boring conferences.'

Fundamentally, networking is about connecting with others – so that occurs just about everywhere on earth! From the bus queue to the tube ride to town, from your local book-store to the supermarket or pub, people to network with are everywhere. For those who prefer to stay at home all day, the internet is their virtual vehicle to connect with others. Networking is not just about attending social events, although those are good opportunities too.

Myth 3: 'Networking is hard work and takes too much time.'

To be effective, networking does take time and work, which is an ongoing process. But this does not mean it's hard. How hard is it for you to spend time with friends? How difficult is it for you to talk about your favourite subject with people who also share your passion?

Brilliant networkers know how to connect effectively, saving themselves a lot of wasted time and helping to reach their goals a lot quicker than those without networks.

Myth 4: 'I'm a senior manager and for me networking is not necessary. I'm already advanced and successful in my career.'

Have you ever heard the expression 'It's lonely at the top'? Well it's probably the biggest lie. Possibly put about to discourage anyone from aspiring to get there. The fact is the more senior a manager you become, the greater your reliance on relationships, and doing things with and through others. The phrase 'the old boy network', signifying senior managers helping their

> brilliant networkers know how to connect effectively

own, is not a recent invention and throughout history people who were in favour with rulers of the time were often the ones that gained power as a result. For leaders in the 21st century being connected is more vital than ever before.

Myth 5: 'I'm too junior to network with those above me and cannot learn from my peers. There is no one suitable for me to network with.'

It might well be that you are not yet on first-name terms with your CEO, and not likely to be so for some time, but there are many tried and tested ways that you can build effective relationships with those above you.

Whether by meeting people at external groups or volunteering for projects that get you exposure outside your immediate team, it's worth thinking about the variety of ways that you can get involved and network with those in more senior positions. This is covered later in the book.

Myth 6: 'I can be successful by working alone. Hard work is all that is necessary.'

Although this is obviously true, and you can be successful through hard work, this work can be made more enjoyable and less onerous if networking principles are used.

Another important point is that, rather than doing it alone, with others you benefit from the value of diversity and gain other people's different perspectives, which you might not have working on a task alone.

The top seven reasons to network

1   Networking is a way to meet new people. Through networking you can find customers, partners, investors, mentors and friends.

2   Networking can provide you with the information you need to make decisions. Often you will find out something you did not know you were looking for.

3   Networking can connect you to expertise and resources – whether you are looking for someone to give you marketing advice for your new business or who will do a house swap with you for the summer.

4   Networking can lead to you getting the job of your dreams, being promoted within your job or making a career move.

5   Networking can help you solve dilemmas and problems and enables you to work with others to find common solutions.

6   Networking can assist you with any goal that can benefit from the support of others. From losing weight to starting your own company, networking can help you achieve all your goals faster by connecting you to people who want to help.

7   Networking allows you to share your experience, and give to others. The communities formed can do everything, from sharing music to using their skills and talents to change the world.

PART 2

The
networking
mindset

CHAPTER 4

Your
networking
goals

One of the main things that distinguishes brilliant networkers from ordinary networkers is that they have a clear idea of what they want to gain from the activities they do. They know what they want. This might simply be to meet new friends. It could be to secure a job or perhaps get a promotion or change career. Maybe you want to meet someone who has inspired you.

Whatever your goal, it helps to be very clear about what you want, so it's useful to identify and set clear goals. Unless you know what you want to achieve from networking, just doing it isn't likely to achieve very much.

A useful analogy for having a goal is taking a journey. Would you leave a station in a taxi and tell the driver to take you somewhere warm, comfortable or interesting rather than giving him an address? Would you be surprised by where you ended up if you did?

If you wanted to travel from Twickenham to Glasgow, would you just get in your car and drive in any direction? No, you would plan your journey, perhaps looking at a map and deciding which route to take.

The same applies to networking. Every time you network you need to know what you want to achieve from the activity. Your goal might be anywhere along the range of developing a friendship to prospecting a customer – but by being clear about what it is that you want, you are more likely to benefit from networking.

brilliant tip

Brilliant networkers have clear goals and are able to identify opportunities as they present themselves, while also being relaxed, going with the flow and not pushing against the river.

Clear directions

The unconscious mind is always searching for a direction in which to take us. We can either tell it directly where we want to go or we can step back, do nothing and let it take us where we intuitively think we should go. The direct action approach is obviously better. It is not only important to have goals but also there is great clarity to be gained in writing them down.

How do I define my networking goals?

There are five steps in this process. If the question is not relevant to your first goal you can skip it and apply it to another of your goals.

Step 1

Write down what it is that *you want*. State this in the positive. For example if the goal is to be slim, rather than saying 'I don't want to be overweight' a better formulation would be 'I want to be my ideal weight'. In the case of networking it might be 'I want a new job'.

Step 2

Write down specifically how you will *know* when you have achieved your goal. What will you see, hear and feel on achieving it? Use as many senses as possible.

> what will you see, hear and feel on achieving it?

For example:

In my new job I will see myself in a clear open-plan environment with natural light and modern furnishings. I will have the title of Marketing Director and three staff will report to me. I will hear the noise of people on the phone, and laughing and talking to each other about their work. I will feel engaged, motivated and loving my job.

Step 3

Is the goal self-initiated and self-maintained? Is it only for you? The answer to this question is yes or no.

Sometimes we are tempted to set goals for others. For example, 'I want Pam to talk to me more'. Whether Pam talks to you more or less is not directly a goal that is focused on what you can initiate or do. It's important when setting goals for networking to concentrate on your own behaviour and actions, not those of others you wish to influence.

brilliant tip

Sometimes we might be asked to network by our boss or company for a specific purpose. In this case the organisation or manager has initiated the networking and would look to see results in its maintenance. If this happens it is important to clarify with your boss and company *how they will know you have been successful and what specific outcome they are looking for.* Make the goals set for you personal by asking yourself the question, 'What do I need to accomplish?'

Step 4

Is the outcome placed in the proper context? What is the new behaviour, in what situations do you want to display it, and where do you want to display it? These questions really focus on the detail, if your goal is looking to behave differently.

Let's say your goal in reading this book is to relate more confidently to other people. Then your answer to this question might be: 'I want to be more confident at work with my boss in asking for a promotion. I want to do this at our bi-weekly meeting.' Note how much clearer this goal is than simply 'I want to be confident'.

Step 5

What would be the results of the change on other areas of your life? Would the change you seek have negative effects on other areas of your life?

When setting a goal it is important to think about what the costs will be as a result of achieving it or whether there is something else that you may have to sacrifice. If you are aware of this when setting your goal, you are more likely to be able to manage it or accept that there are costs as well as benefits to your decision. The alternative could be unconscious sabotage, where you inadvertently create reasons not to achieve your goal. For example, the cost of having new friends might mean that you could end up spending less time with your partner. This might have a negative impact on your relationship, so it is important that you get the balance right when increasing your friendships and the activities these involve.

Applying the five steps

Now take a few moments to record what goals you want networking to bring you. Identify the top three goals you want to achieve while reading this book. You might apply the five steps above to ensure they are well-formed outcomes.

In thinking about what you want, you could complete the sentence: 'I want networking to bring me the following benefits ...'

My goals as a result of reading *Brilliant networking* are:

1.

2.

3.

For example:

My goals as a result of reading *Brilliant networking* are:

1. *To find a new job.*

2. *To meet a new partner with similar interests.*

3. *To have a wider social network.*

Two ideas to keep your goals in mind

Affirmations

Writing down what you want to achieve specifically is key to your success but it is easy to forget what your goals are on a daily basis. A useful way to remind yourself of your goals is to use affirmations – statements which are written down.

There are three factors that must be present to make an affirmation effective. These are the three Ps: they must be **personal, positive** and **present**:

- By 'personal' it means that the affirmation should have the personal pronoun 'I'.

- By 'positive' it should be stated how you want the event to happen and what you want.

- By 'present' it means that you state it as if you have achieved your goal *now*.

For example: 'It is 1 July 2011 and I have a new job.'

brilliant example

Pink elephants

You might ask, 'Why do I need to state my goals in the positive?' If I now asked you *not* to think of a pink elephant chasing a policeman, then in order for you *not* to think about it, your mind first has to create the image and then delete it. The unconscious mind cannot process negatives as easily as it can process positives. There is a story about an American factory where one working area was dangerous and workmen kept on slipping. In order to improve the situation the foreman decided to put a **Don't Slip** sign in the area. After a few months with the new sign, the management discovered that more people had industrial accidents owing to slipping on the site than before the sign was put up! The foreman should have put up a sign saying **Take Care** – which is positive.

It is important that the goals in the affirmation are realistically achievable. If I was to say, 'It is 15 July 2011 and I have a million pounds in my bank account', this would be out of line with where I am at present and also incongruent with where I have set my other goals relating to work and leisure. By using the five steps exercise you will ensure your goals and affirmations are well thought out.

At the same time it is important not to aim too low. Your past does not determine your future success. If you aim much higher than average you will have to develop the new skills and techniques needed to achieve this, rather than if you had aimed only slightly higher.

> it is important not to aim too low

No matter where you scored on the networking quiz, by aiming to be a brilliant networker you set yourself up to make that possible.

For each of your networking goals create a positive affirmation regarding your outcome.

brilliant tip

Some people find it very useful to write out their affirmations a number of times in the morning or before bed each day. As they do this they allow themselves to imagine successfully achieving their goals. By making this a habit they keep focused on their goals and think positively about them.

Testimonials

Another tool for keeping your goal in mind is to write testimonials as if you have achieved your goal. These are similar to the testimonials of thanks made by satisfied customers in newspaper or magazine adverts. By doing this you create a clear mental picture of having achieved your goal and as a consequence it seems more possible – because you have achieved it, mentally at least, which is an important first stage. You are creating a blueprint for your goal. It is important to have fun with this and let your imagination go, both of which reinforce the positive.

To write your testimonial:

1   Be positive and use the present tense – write with the successful outcome in mind as if it has already happened.

2   Problem to solution – write how it used to be and how things are different now.

3   Sensory rich – convey your feelings and use the senses in vividly describing your success.

4   When you have finished your testimonial keep it safe, perhaps in a journal or other place where you record your private thoughts. You could put it in an envelope and future date the testimonial. Do not open it till after the date has passed and hopefully you will not be surprised to find you have achieved your goal!

▶ brilliant example

Below is a testimonial for the goal of making more friends. You can address the testimonial to someone you think would be delighted at the news: Enveloped marked 1 March 2011.

Dear Ben,

Since reading and putting into practice the principles and techniques in Brilliant networking, *my friendships have increased dramatically, not only in quantity but also in quality. In December last year I had two close friends that I spent little time with as they were often busy with their families. All this changed when I decided to focus on renewing friendships that I had let slip and also to start activities that I found enjoyable and fun in themselves, which for me was acting in our local theatre company. Since then I have made at least half a dozen new friends that I see two or three times a week and we have great conversations – not only about who got to play the lead!*

Steven

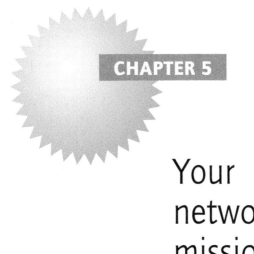

CHAPTER 5

Your networking mission

eyond short-term tactical goals, if you have a deeper vision that is aligned to your goals you will have a powerful tool to become a brilliant networker. People are drawn to others who have a clear mission, purpose or vision. Often this is translated into a *passion* or a *cause* that is bigger than themselves. It is this 'cause' that engages people and captivates them.

In business we have seen over the past decade a rise in 'cause-related marketing'. This is when a business markets itself through the idea that by buying its product you can also benefit a charity or a worthy cause: for example, shop at Tesco and we will buy computers for your child's school. While these schemes have their detractors they are positive to consumers who are attracted by the bigger purpose of 'cause' beyond the benefits of the product.

brilliant example

A friend of mine was telling me about a young man in a wheelchair. He lost his legs at 19 but was determined to lead a full and active life. He had a wheelchair that enabled him to do that. Yet he knew from his research that there were over 100 million people who had lost legs in the world but did not have wheelchairs to give them mobility. He made it his mission to network with people to achieve a wheelchair for as many of these 100 million people as possible. He used his vision and took action, exploring manufacturing the wheelchairs at low cost in China where he developed the design and process.

He might never achieve all these wheelchairs but he was able to gather the support of everyone at a large conference he spoke at where he declared his vision. A multi-millionaire who was at the event was so moved he immediately pledged 25 per cent of his profits towards the project.

This young man's purpose and his mission gave him a compelling reason to network. We might not have the same goal as him but I suggest that we should all develop a compelling reason to network.

brilliant tip

Brilliant networkers always have a compelling reason to reach out and connect. This might be a project they are working on, or bringing together a group of people to make a difference. Providing a compelling reason for others to connect with you automatically makes it easier for people to say yes.

Mission or purpose statements

One of the trends in companies across the world is to have statements that describe what they do, 'their purpose', which often includes the way they do it. Sometimes this is called a 'mission statement', sometimes simply 'our purpose' or 'vision'. A key change in management thinking was the recognition that not only can companies have brands, but people too. Their brand is what they are known by others to be like. This can encompass their attitudes, behaviours and tastes but also reliability, trustworthiness and ability to do business.

> not only can companies have brands, but people too

Some individuals are used as brands because customers and potential customers know what they stand for and what they symbolise. These personal brands are then used by companies to endorse other brands in order to drive sales: for example, David Beckham is used by many brands for his fashion style and reputation as a sports icon. It is no accident that advertisers cleverly use celebrity endorsements to symbolise the benefits of their products and to influence customers to choose their brand over another.

Identify what you stand for and what is important to you

Discovering our purpose is often a lifelong task. It is unlikely we will hear the voice of God booming into our ear telling us, 'This is what you must do'. More often it is rather the small, quiet and persistent whisperings of our feelings and experience that reveal our purpose to us.

brilliant definition

Your personal brand is the whole and complete message you give to others about yourself beyond just the rhetoric.

Work through the following questions, listing your answers on a separate sheet of paper, and see what they trigger:

1 What is really important to you?

2 If you won the lottery and didn't have to work one more day, what would you do with your time?

3 What do you enjoy doing so much that you 'lose yourself' in the activity and it gives you energy?

4 What persistent complaints or upsets do you hear about that you would like to take action on?

5 How would you say that you are different to others?

6 What qualities do you admire in others that you would like to display? (Think of specific people and write about their qualities.)

7 What do you want others to say about you? (A useful exercise here is to imagine that it is your funeral and that somebody is telling the mourners about your life, your character and what was important to you.)

Once you have done this try writing out your qualities and thoughts in a statement about yourself below. Don't worry if you cannot write in the form of a statement. Just answering the above questions will have made you more aware of what it is that you value and what you feel you can contribute to others.

Let's say my personal values are inspiration, integrity and gener-osity. It would make no sense for me to be dishonest with people and selfish, as clearly there would

> clear values allow people to trust me

be a conflict with my values. Having a sense of my own values will help me discriminate, knowing what opportunities to take and what I might choose to pass on. It would also let me know the kind of people that I would like to interact with and those I choose to have further interactions with. More importantly, clear values allow people to trust me, trust being vital to any long-term relationship.

In his book *The Speed of Trust* (2006), Covey points to trust being the vital differentiator in the new economy. Trust is built by keeping agreements and promises, being courteous, etc. In the bestselling book, *The Seven Habits of Highly Effective People* (1999), this was portrayed through the analogy of an emotional bank account.

The theory is that with every relationship there is a balance account built, similar to a bank account, that illustrates how much you have both put into the relationship or taken out. When we do something positive (e.g. remember a name, say thank you, keep a promise) we build trust, hence our bank account deposit with that person is higher. If we did some-thing wrong, 'take a withdrawal', this probably would not break or seriously damage the relationship if there is already a strong balance.

Conversely the opposite is also true. If withdrawals consist-ently occur without enough positive deposits it is unlikely that trust will develop and we could lose that friendship or relation-ship. Our values are communicated in the same way through our behaviour.

brilliant tip

When thinking about your values it is important to see how often you can build them into your relationship when networking.
Ask yourself the question, 'In what ways can I demonstrate what I stand for?', and then do it. Actions speak loudest.

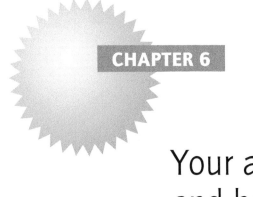

CHAPTER 6

Your attitudes
and beliefs

n his bestselling book, *The Inner Game of Tennis* (1972), (tennis coach) W. Timothy Gallwey broadened the focus on the way that results were obtained in competitive tennis. He discovered that success on the tennis court was not only about focusing on the external skills that everybody could see, but that the internal skills of confidence, resilience, mental attitude, 'letting go' and being in a state of flow were equally important. His experience showed that it was the 'psychology of champions' that made the difference, especially when external skills were similar.

Attitudes and beliefs come before tools and techniques

Put simply, our values and beliefs directly shape our actions, which then become habits that lead to success or failure in networking. For example, if I believe that 'I am not a confident person', this belief could result in choosing activities where there is no need for interaction with others. Doing things alone then becomes a habit, and, without interaction, networking is impossible.

However, if I simply changed my behaviour and tried to be in a group of people, while still believing that I was not a confident person, I would feel uncomfortable, and this would reinforce my belief that I would be better off alone. It is not enough just to change behaviour, you also have to change your beliefs.

Be prepared to take a risk

Most of us, at different times, have felt like Wallflower Wanda. We have probably looked at Connecting Carole and wondered whether we were both from the same planet. How could two people be so different in their ability to connect? Being 'pain-fully' shy does guarantee a few things. It benefits us that we do not have to communicate. We therefore avoid any embarrassment, confrontation or awkwardness. Yet on the other side of the coin, there is a cost. The cost is that we might never benefit from the connection, fulfilment or joy that truly connecting with another person brings. Opportunity comes with a risk.

opportunity comes
with a risk

By being open to meeting new people and connecting, you are equally open to rejection. Yet skilled networkers know that this is far outweighed by the benefits of any possible connection. Brilliant networkers believe people are generally friendly and would welcome connection.

Change your beliefs

One of the most powerful ways you can set yourself up for networking success is to change your limited beliefs about networking. The importance of attitude can be illustrated by the 'bad day' example.

Have you ever had one of those days when *everything* seemed to go wrong? First you did not wake up on time when you needed to get to that interview... perhaps you missed an important meeting... or forgot to call your colleague on her birthday... just missed your bus and then it started raining... walked to the pub to discover they had just called last orders! Even if some things went well, in this state, you did not notice them.

Sometimes when we are feeling in a particular mood every-thing around us seems to confirm our belief. If we believe we are foolish and someone criticises us we would use that as firm evidence to prove we are right in our negative belief.

This is true even in the opposite. Have you ever been so happy that no matter what went on in the day... people were late... you missed the bus... but you just did not care. You were happy and nothing could make you sad! Even if someone criticised you, you would probably still be happy.

Believe in what you do

The first step is to *become conscious* about your beliefs. Many of our beliefs are *unconscious* and even though we may deny we believe them with our words, our actions tell a different story. Once you have identified those negative beliefs that could sab-otage your attempts to network, you can begin the process of re-evaluating those beliefs, rejecting them and creating positive ones. We may not be able to create outside reality but we do have a say in our own internal experience of this reality.

brilliant impact

Changing your beliefs about your capacity to network is one of the primary keys to success. Your behaviour and results always reflect what you really believe.

CHAPTER 7

Your
confidence

T o explore your beliefs about networking do the following:

1. Write down five reasons why you believe you _can_ network easily:

1

2

3

4

5

2. Now write down all the reasons why you believe that you _cannot_, at present, network easily:

(e.g. _I can't make small talk._)

1

2

3

4

5

6

7

8

3. For each of the reasons recorded in answer to part 2 write down answers to the following four questions in the box opposite.

I will use the belief 'I am not confident' as an example.

Q1 How would you know if this belief wasn't true?

I would not feel so shy in approaching people. If I was invited to an event I would be feeling happy rather than having feelings of dread.

Q2 Do you know of **any examples at all** where or when this belief is **not** true?

Well, it's not true with my family or my best friend. With them I feel confident and am not at all shy.

Q3 I know you believe this belief to be true but what would happen if this belief was not true? How would you **be** if the opposite was the case? What would you be **seeing**, **hearing**, **feeling** and **doing**?

I would be feeling confident inside when I am approaching people, or being approached. I would notice myself smiling, that my body is relaxed and my breathing regular. I would hear myself talking confidently and listening intently. I would see interest on the face of those I am talking to as they carefully listen to what I am saying.

Q4 What do you **now believe instead** since the old belief is no longer true?

I believe that sometimes I can be confident. I am confident with people close to me and have the potential to be confident and relaxed with others.

Reason 1

Q1

Q2

Q3

Q4

Reason 2

Q1

Q2

Q3

Q4

Reason 3

Q1

Q2

Q3

Q4

Reason 4

Q1

Q2

Q3

Q4

brilliant tip

Even finding one example of when a belief is not true prevents it from being a universal belief. In conversation we tend to use a lot of universal beliefs denoted by the words 'all', 'everyone', 'all the time', 'never'. For example, 'He never thanks me'. By questioning the universal belief and finding one example we prove that the belief is not true and we have the possibility of a new belief: 'Sometimes he thanks me.'

Having done this process for each of your limiting beliefs you might begin to notice, straightaway, or perhaps after a little while, how easy it is for you to have the belief that *you can confidently network*. You might take your answer to Q3 and turn it into a positive affirmation: for example, 'I feel confident inside when approaching people'.

Perhaps you had those beliefs that limited you in the past because you did not have a model that allowed you to explore all the factors that contribute to your understanding that *you have the ability to network successfully*.

brilliant impact

Limiting beliefs tend to become self-fulfilling prophecies. So do positive beliefs. For the next seven days, notice how people's **language reflects their beliefs**.

Practise eliminating from your language the following phrases:

- I can't...
- It's OK for him/her but...
- I'm no good...
- Things just don't go my way...
- I'll fail...etc...etc...

Even if you think they are true, **they are only beliefs**.

Instead substitute them with the following phrases:

- I can...
- I'll find a way...
- I can learn...
- I am good at this...
- Things go my way...
- If they can do it, so can I...
- I will succeed...

These are also beliefs but the crucial difference is that they **set you up for success**.

The secret to having the confidence to network is to develop strong positive beliefs and to question your limiting beliefs.

Get the confidence

There are countless tips for developing self-confidence but the essential point is that this confidence is not made up of just one thing. It is made up of *self-respect* and *self-worth* and *self-esteem*. Self-confidence could be thought of as a continuum. In our day-to-day lives we move through different emotions relevant to the situations we find ourselves in, rather than being shy or being extremely confident all the time.

> self-confidence could be thought of as a continuum

Julia Hastings, author of *You're Great* (1995), writes about ways you can control your emotions in various situations through visualisation techniques that you can practise before you go out and meet others.

One of the techniques is to imagine putting on an invisible jacket that glitters in gold and says 'VIP' across your chest. When you do this in reality, take the time to create the scene in your mind. Make the picture brighter and more colourful. How does it feel to be wearing a jacket that says you're a VIP? Now imagine meeting people who notice that you are a VIP. Notice how they treat you with admiration and respect. How you convey this authority even without the jacket that says 'I am special'. Notice how comfortable you feel around others and meeting and being introduced to strangers. The trick is that when you do go to an event you can put on (in your imagination) your VIP jacket and gain all the confidence you need.

Other visualisations Julia goes through are imagining wearing a T-shirt that has the word 'Irresistible' across your chest. Feel the confidence that this brings – especially with those of the opposite sex! Another technique is to imagine that everyone is coming to you and you have people literally eating from your hands! Here you would imagine birdseed and people coming to you and eating the seed. Notice that you feel completely calm and in control.

Have fun with these techniques. Enjoy the feelings they give you and know that when you want to recapture the feeling you can, just by using your imagination. Using imagination is fun but, as demonstrated above, there is a definite connection between your thoughts, your body and the impact imagination has to boost confidence!

> imagining yourself as a nervous wreck will hardly boost your confidence

A second use of imagery is to imagine the actual situation in which you have to network as being a film. This time you imagine the people you will meet, the venue, etc. and see the outcome as desired. With your confidence to approach people, you will be able to hold good conversations. The key is that the mental rehearsals must have a positive outcome! It goes without saying that imagining yourself as a nervous wreck will hardly boost your confidence.

Whichever option you choose, really make the images sensory rich. For example, you might imagine going to a party and shaking someone's hand. Notice how they smile and how relaxed and confident you feel. You might notice some of the detail in the room and how you are breathing slowly and deeply, enjoying the great conversation. Try to notice details like the feel of the clothes on your back, the smell of the leather furniture. Just pretend. The more detail that you can bring in about what you do know will be true of the event – for example some of the people who will be there, the venue – will all help to make it more real. This also creates a future blueprint – on the night it will go so smoothly you will think it is déjà vu.

brilliant tip

Ordinary practices bring ordinary results. Extraordinary practices create extraordinary results. Practise the techniques in this chapter and you will be surprised by your positive results.

CHAPTER 8

Your
motivation

f you are still reading this book, you are already demonstrating a key skill of a brilliant networker: persistence. And behind persistence lies motivation. You want to find out how to network, and how to network effectively. If you have put into practice the earlier exercises you now know where you are going, you have a clear purpose and, perhaps more importantly, the confidence and tools to create the self-belief that will get you there. Yet even if you do know what you want, there may still be barriers that stop you going out there and doing it. Does the following sound familiar?

It's 6.30 on Wednesday evening, you have just got back from work and are flopped on the couch. You feel so comfortable that to lie there is the *only* thing you can do! You've been invited to a book club by a friend at work. Surely, you think, they won't miss you. You fall asleep on the couch and the next day you forget to ask your friend about her evening. You see her later in the day and she tells you how great the evening was and how many interesting people were there who shared your interests.

It might not be a book club. It could have been a party, a work event or even a dinner with friends – but sometimes we can miss opportunities because we didn't have the motivation to take them.

While meeting others and networking is not hard work, it does sometimes take motivation to do something or go somewhere when we would rather be at home. The trick is to get a balance, focus on what matters most, but to make sure that you don't pass up on too many invitations that might create good opportunities to network.

> **brilliant** tip
>
> Often the most resilient are the most successful, because they pass the first requirement for success – showing up.

this antidote is called *motivation*

A common factor for not taking action in networking is a potential killer – *procrastination* – putting off what we have to do. Yet there is an antidote to procrastination that you can develop. This antidote is called *motivation.*

The meaning of motivation

Motivation is a propulsion for your behaviour to achieve a particular goal. If very strong it manifests as a burning desire within you that is unstoppable. When you are really motivated to do something... really motivated... and take action... you will be more likely to achieve it. On the other hand there is 'weak' motivation, which can be construed as a mere wish or desire without the strong emotional attachment to the outcome.

↗ brilliant impact

The strength of our motivation can be betrayed by our language. Look at this scale of motivation for 'networking':

I **could** network – just a possibility.

I **should** network – weak, as not intrinsic motivation.

I **would** like to network – weak wish, just an expression of interest.

I **have** to network – stronger but not compelling enough.

I **must** network – strongest if self-initiated and maintained.

By creating a 'must act' attitude we develop the capacity to take action.

There are two basic types of motivation that we can use to develop a 'must act' motivation:

● towards motivation

● away-from motivation.

Towards motivation

As the word 'towards' indicates, this motivation is *in order to get* to a particular goal or something you desire. For example, a towards motivation might be, 'I want to be slim', and you move towards being a particular weight. In networking, a towards motivation might be, 'I want to meet a potential employer', or 'I want to be more confident'.

Away-from motivation

This motivation is not so much towards a goal but away from something that you do not want, doing something *in order not to get* a consequence. In slimming, people are motivated sometimes to begin diets *not* because they want to be healthy but because they *do not want* to be overweight and experience all the feelings that come with their unwanted state. In networking, you might be motivated to stay at home because you *do not want* to experience being in a group of people you are unfamiliar with, rather than wanting to stay at home for positive reasons.

Developing your motivation

How would it be for you if you felt really motivated to network? If you felt relaxed and looked forward to meeting new people, connecting and sharing information?

This is possible – and here is an exercise to develop your own motivation.

Step 1: Discover how you are motivated

Can you remember a time when you felt *really really* motivated to do something and you completed it successfully? *Be there now in your imagination.*

Why were you motivated? What was motivating you in this situation?

If your answer is positive and indicates what you wanted, you have a **towards** motivation strategy. If the answer indicates what you did not want, you have an **away-from** motivation strategy.

> use a strategy that is towards what you do want

The secret to self-motivation is to use a strategy that is towards what you do want. If you use an away-from motivation strategy you will tend to attract the negative conditions back into your life, which will demotivate you again. This explains why some people become millionaires and go broke several times over. Their initial drive was to escape poverty, yet in wealth the motivation was quickly lost.

Step 2: Motivate yourself towards success

I want you now to imagine having successfully completed a task you selected for yourself. It is finished and you did it really well. What are all the **good consequences you might experience as a result?**

For example:

I attended the business conference with the senior management team. We had a great evening and discovered we had so much in common. My daughter goes to the school my manager is trying to get her daughter into so I offered advice on the selection process. This was really well received and we have become good friends. At work I have been given important projects and am due for a promotion.

What **will** you be **seeing, hearing, feeling, having, doing** and **being** in a **month's** time, just from having completed this task successfully? Really intensify your imagination. Make it big, bright, colourful, and once you have a picture add sound, touch and taste. Really imagine enjoying the success that you have now achieved in relation to your chosen task.

For example:

It's one month later and I am regularly invited to meetings with the senior management team. I have been brought onto cross-functional teams and given more responsibility for important tasks. At the weekend I meet with some of the other senior managers and we have excellent relationships both in and out of the workplace. I feel confident and secure in my job and hear positive feedback.

Now, what are all the **amazing, brilliant, fantastic** things you will be experiencing **one year** from now **having successfully completed the task you did feel motivated about?** Intensify the imagination and be as creative as you want.

For example:

It has been one year from the first business conference and I am now promoted to a senior management grade. I earn nearly a third more in salary than at the beginning of the year, I have a wide network of friends at work and am a respected senior manager.

Finally, in **five years'** time how much **more happiness and joy** have you got as a result of having successfully completed your task? **Relax and feel how happy you are now that you have achieved your task set five years ago.**

For example:

It has now been five years and I enjoy a tremendous life, all starting from a business conference five years ago that I decided to attend. In five years I have been promoted twice. I now head an entire business division.

brilliant tip

If possible always try to choose networking opportunities based around your interests that you genuinely enjoy doing. If you enjoy the process, the results will follow. You will need no help in motivation. If you are doing something you do not enjoy, then the above motivation strategies could be useful.

CHAPTER 9

Share your goals

Have you ever thought, 'I wish I knew someone who knew about X'? Well, you probably do, or you know someone who knows someone who does – that is the basis of networking. But they need to know what it is you are trying to find out about, or what help you need, before they know what to offer you.

The most common cause of failure in our efforts, whether in business, socially or domestically, is failing to share our goals and to ask for help. The lone ranger mentality – 'I can do it alone' – sometimes arises out of fear of failure, but also from possessiveness, or a feeling of not wanting to be seen to be unable to manage a task alone.

> one way to network is to share

This can be unhelpful in the long run, and counterproductive when it comes to networking. One way to network and to advance our own goals is to share.

Be generous

One of the key qualities of brilliant networkers is that they have an 'abundance mentality'. They give of themselves and this giving then attracts a form of repayment, or reciprocity. One could be cynical and describe this as a 'give to get' mentality but often the way it plays out with successful networkers is that they give knowing that sometimes they will not get, but they still enjoy the feeling of giving and do it anyway. Their generosity of spirit encourages others to be generous also.

People generally like to help, and will often go out of their way to be of service. But often they do not know their help is needed. The problem is that we do not ask for help clearly enough or that we do not know where to go for assistance.

▶ brilliant example

I recently worked with a group of university students and got them to do an exercise where they wrote their goal in the top right corner of a sheet of paper and their name on the bottom left and joined this with an arrow. Then along the arrow each immediate step was listed that was needed in order to achieve their goal. For example, Kerry put as her goal she wanted to be a pilot. So one of the steps was 'To find a suitable flying school to take lessons'. Paul had a goal to open a business in China where he was going next year and so he put as one of his steps along that route 'To learn more about retail'.

Each of the 20 or so students put their papers on the ground, sharing their goals and the steps they needed to take, and they walked around looking at everyone else's goals. If they could see an action or step they could assist with, they would put their name by the item and say in a sentence how they could help.

What was astounding was how many resources were available to the group, about which they had no idea beforehand. For example, one of the other students had a brother who had passed his flying test and could give advice. There was another student who shared her retail contacts and who knew a successful retailing contact in China to pass on to Paul.

If we share our goals we are significantly more likely to achieve them than if we do not.

brilliant timesaver

Asking for help is a brilliant timesaver. Using it occasionally and reciprocally does not denote weakness but rather illustrates openness to feedback and to learning from others. Over the next week practise asking for help at least three times. It could be for something small, such as help with the washing, or something big, like a connection that you always wanted from somebody. It doesn't matter whether the answer is positive or not, you are developing your asking muscle and hence your ability to network just by asking!

PART 3

Building your network

CHAPTER 10

Find your network

The TRACKER model

A common misconception of networking is that it is only a business tool. The TRACKER model is a useful model for describing the varied purposes of networking and range of options available to you. This model was developed by Bobo West (**www.bobowest. com**) and the acronym is made up as follows:

- **T**ransactions – buying, selling, getting a job, getting a contract, advertising, etc.
- **R**elationships – business, music, friendship, romance, hobbies, college, etc.
- **A**wareness – campaigns, aid, human rights, climate change, politics, etc.
- **C**are – medical, recovery programmes, mental health, self-help, etc.
- **K**nowledge – learning networks, research, personal development, etc.
- **E**ntertainment – music, video, sports, etc.
- **R**eligion and spirituality – online religious practice, religious groups, spiritual paths, etc.

Mind Map

Another useful technique is the Mind Map, developed by Tony Buzan. Mind Maps provide useful visual representations that allow you to see links and clusters of information more clearly.

Exercise

Take a sheet of A4 paper, turn it landscape, and write your name in the centre within a circle. Then coming from you as a spoke from the centre put a link called 'family' with immediate members of your family coming off from this. See the illustration opposite. Then see how many other direct links you have to you. There could be spokes for people you know from work, church, hobbies or clubs. Once you have done your immediate connections see if you can bridge further to capture the people that these people know. For example, my brother Selwyn is a first link to me. His friend Baljeet would be linked to Selwyn. Baljeet's wife Randeep would be linked to Baljeet. You might choose just to explore how many links you can identify down any one trail. At the end of this exercise you should have a map of the people closest to you.

brilliant tip

If you are focusing on one area, for example business, it might be worth constructing a map for all those who you have business relationships with and seeing how you could also connect people within your network to each other. See if you can spot clusters of people or if you can group them into further divisions.

Mindmapping software

If your network is quite large, or if it is quite dynamic, mapping it on paper has its limitations. There are various mindmapping software programs available. One of the best is MindManager. You can build a network map starting with a set of groupings in your life. Once you have set up your categories you could then begin to focus on each group, as shown here with the Family group.

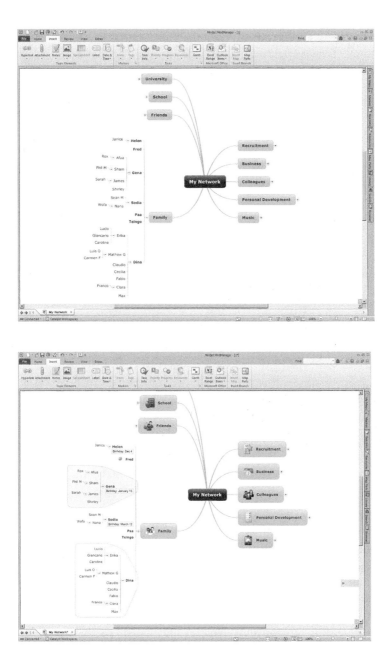

The various other groups could be developed to include new connections as below.

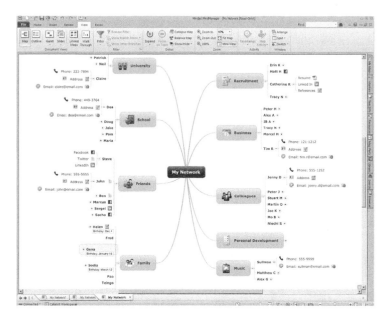

Each contact can be annotated to describe its network relevance. MindManager is rich in features that allow you to add text notes, hyperlinks, colour, visual effects and relationship links. You can then also search by filter, colour, icon, text, etc. This is very powerful and allows you to interrogate and navigate complex networks with relative ease and, most importantly, it is custom-ised for you. You can also export your map to Microsoft Office software (Word, PowerPoint, Project, Visio, Outlook) at the click of a button. The possibilities are virtually limitless, and the latest versions are quite astonishing in their functionality.

Another great piece of software is called The Brain. This is not as feature-rich as MindManager but is more flexible in terms of representing relationships dynamically.

Strong and weak ties

In networking, one of the distinctions that people have made relating to connections is the difference between 'strong ties' – those that you have a direct connection to – and 'weak ties' – those to whom you are connected through others, not directly.

What psychologists discovered was that, surprisingly, 'weak ties' could be more helpful than 'strong ties' in helping you achieve your goals. Why is this? Primarily because people with whom you have strong ties generally share the same interests as you. They only know the same or many of the same people as you, and would probably only have access to similar resources or information as you. On the other hand 'weak ties' know people that you

> 'weak ties' could be more helpful than 'strong ties'

do not, they have access to possible experiences outside your sphere and could have information or resources that are not within your reach. This diversity does much to enrich your network, so it is well worth thinking about.

More than 25% of people who find jobs through networking receive the referral from someone they meet once a year or less.

University of Dublin, Trinity College, Careers Advisory Service

The trick to maximising this is for you to connect with as many weak ties as possible – people with whom you do not have a strong relationship – but to do it through strong ties if possible. People who can connect you to others are called *connectors*.

The connectors

Essentially, connectors do not have direct access to information, but they act almost as mediators or brokers connecting people for mutual benefit.

An example of a connector is the 'matchmaker'. In order to bring the perfect couple together, the skilled matchmaker would have to be trusted by both the possible future partners. She would have to know their preferences, their likes and dislikes, and be able to make a decision based on what would work for both parties. Once connected, the matchmaker would step out of the relationship and the two partners, at least in this story, would live happily ever after.

From your network map, try to establish who are the connectors available to you, who could let your request be known to a third party. Additionally, try to identify how there might also be value to them through this connection.

It is an interesting phenomenon that through connectors we can reach almost anybody that we wish. This led to a theory called 'six degrees of separation' (see box). If the theory is true, to use it practically you just need to send your request to the person you think most likely to be able to take it forward and then the chain begins.

Six degrees of separation

Six degrees of separation is the theory that anyone on the planet can be connected to any other person on the planet through a chain of acquaintances that has no more than five intermediaries.
The theory was first proposed in 1929 by the Hungarian writer Frigyes Karinthy in a short story called 'Chains'.

In 1967, American sociologist Stanley Milgram devised a new way to test the theory, which he called 'the small-world problem'.
He randomly selected people in the mid-West to send packages to a

stranger located in Massachusetts. The senders knew the recipient's name, occupation and general location. They were instructed to send the package to a person they knew on a first-name basis who they thought was most likely, out of all their friends, to know the target personally. That person would do the same, and so on, until the package was personally delivered to its target recipient.

Although the participants expected the chain to include at least 100 intermediaries, it only took (on average) between five and seven intermediaries to get each package delivered. Milgram's findings were published in *Psychology Today* and inspired the phrase 'six degrees of separation'. Although his findings were discounted after it was discovered that he based his conclusion on a very small number of packages, six degrees of separation became an accepted notion in popular culture.

In 2001, Duncan Watts, a professor at Columbia University, continued his own earlier research into the phenomenon and recreated Milgram's experiment on the internet. Watts used an e-mail message as the 'package' that needed to be delivered, and surprisingly, after reviewing the data collected by 48,000 senders and 19 targets (in 157 countries), Watts found that the average number of intermediaries was indeed six.

CHAPTER 11

Networking groups

One of the most frequent structured ways you can network is through the use of networking groups. These vary from 'business related groups' with the emphasis on doing business or promoting your company and products, to 'social networking' sites where the emphasis is more on sharing information or building social relationships. Whether online or face-to-face it is important that you choose the right groups or forums to join.

brilliant **timesaver**

Ask yourself the following questions before you commit to any network:

1　Is the group related to your target goal for networking? Remember to identify your purpose in networking. Your membership of each group will have a different goal, but does it bring you closer to the goal you've identified?

2　Is the group organiser willing to share information beforehand about who will attend the meeting or event? If this is not offered you should always request it. This will allow you to decide whether you want to attend a particular meeting and allow you vital preparation or save you time if there is no one that you wish to connect with.

3   Is attendance compulsory at all meetings or can you just attend those you want to? This is important as sometimes membership of an organisation is dependent on consistent attendance, even when this does not make valuable use of your time.

4   Is membership good value for money? If the group costs £100 a year to join but only has two meetings a year that you feel are relevant to your needs, is this the best use of your money? If the networking organisers are happy to connect you to an existing member to discuss how they have benefited, this is a good way to discover if this is a forum for you.

5   How much of your time and maintenance will a particular networking opportunity take? We could be networking all day if need be, but will it bring you closer to your goals? Do you really want to be online all day keeping up links and posting your comments on blogs?

A large part of choosing the right forum for you will depend on your personal style. A lot of people find the prospect of face-to-face networking intimidating and prefer technology as a means to connect on a much wider scale. Yet often face-to-face contact, removing the PC between parties, allows for a much deeper connection.

It is worth bearing in mind that although relationships can start online, including dating relationships, they ultimately end up face-to-face at some point if the relationship continues.

Face-to-face networks

Below are some of the groups through which you can access networking opportunities:

● local community groups
● Chambers of Commerce/ Junior Chambers of Commerce

- industry bodies
- professional associations
- in-company employee networks
- membership of clubs, including networking clubs
- conferences/speakers' events.

This list is by no means exhaustive and hence the need to be clear about your networking goals in order to choose the groups that are best for you.

Another way to source networks is to look in industry journals and trade publications where groups or meetings are advertised. Opportunities might also occur at conferences where people are asked if they want to share their details and connect with the rest of the group. Sometimes it is just worth asking individuals for recommendations of people to approach or groups to join, or to go along to one session to see if this makes sense for you to participate in the longer term.

brilliant tip

Another way to find out what events and meetings are happening within your industry is to sign up for newsletters. These often contain useful information featuring people and success stories and often are free. To avoid an overload of free newsletters, create a separate, free e-mail address for industry newsletters so you keep your personal e-mail private. Identify the five or six leading groups or professional bodies in your industry and subscribe.

What happens at a group or networking event?

Here I turn to an expert, Damien Senn. After starting his own internet business, he began a search for other passionate, inspired people and established 'Web Wednesdays', a networking and support group for other internet entrepreneurs.

The club meets on a monthly basis and attracts a wide variety of people interested in the internet. The events are very informal and there is no pressure to meet anyone. People just mingle and talk to the people they want to about anything they want to. Nothing is ever forced. The fascinating thing about this approach to networking is that, according to Damien, you always seem to end up talking to the very people you need to.

Below are Damien's tips for networking success at group events.

brilliant tips

1   *You get out what you put in!*
    This is the number one rule for making the most out of your networking evening! If you sit back and wait for other people to approach you, you're not going to get much out of it. Remember that this is intended to be a friendly and supportive environment. Take the initiative, introduce yourself to some new people and, most important of all, enjoy yourself!

2   *Be yourself.*
    You don't have to be anyone other than yourself. Be genuine and others will appreciate you for who you are. It doesn't matter what stage you're at as long as you have a keen desire to develop and grow. The people in attendance will have different levels of experience, ranging from newbies starting out all the way up to experienced, but all have something to offer.

3 *Take a genuine interest in other people.*
One of the real key secrets to networking is taking a genuine interest in other people. When you truly listen and understand where another person is coming from you are in a much better position to help them along on their journey, or know what they could help you with. And the more you help other people, the more they will be willing to help you!

4 *Share your knowledge, resources and contacts.*
Come along with an abundant mindset. Share your resources, knowledge and contacts and do your best to make the evening a worthwhile experience for everyone that you meet. And remember, one of the secrets of life is that the more you give, the more you receive.

5 *Know your goals for the evening.*
This is crucial. Come along to each session with a clear idea about what you would like to get out of it. Maybe you would like to have a specific question answered or even a new joint venture partner. If you are clear about your goals, both present and future, you are more likely to attract the people who can help you.

6 *Bring your business cards.*
Make sure you come prepared with business cards to pass out to people who you'd like to keep in contact with. Be sure to include your name, phone number, e-mail address and website domain if you have one. If you don't already have a business card, lots of high street print shops or stationers have business card print facilities.

7 *Come regularly.*
Let's face it, no one can truly run a successful business on their own. We all need help and guidance along the way. Relationships, contacts and networks are crucial to your success, so come along regularly!

CHAPTER 12

Networking in the virtual community

S haring information is key to networking, and one of the greatest revolutions in recent years is the use of online opportunities and access to virtual communities. For younger generations this is the norm, but others may need to learn how to use and exploit virtual opportunities.

Richard Lockyer, personal coach, kindly contributed his experience to the following section.

Blogs

A blog (short for web log) started out a bit like an online diary but over time has evolved into much more than this as it developed and expanded to meet people's needs. As of September 2009, there were estimated to be over 125 million blogs in existence, so blogging is a great way to network.

Now considered to be an important tool to have in your marketing arsenal, blogs are used by individuals as online diaries or a place to air views on any subject that you can think of.

Once you have set up your blog, you need to start telling

> a great way to start is by 'pinging' your blog

people that you are up and running and that you want to hear from them. A great way to start is by 'pinging' your blog. This means telling search engines that you have updated your blog.

They then pick up on that and give your blog a higher ranking, which makes it easier to find if someone is searching for a subject that is contained in your blog.

On any blog, there is an area where people can come and leave comments, just as you can on theirs, and in doing so they also leave the URLs to their sites. People see these, visit their sites and so bring other strands to the network.

Access other people's blogs and leave your comments with your URL. If people like what they see they will follow your URL and very quickly you have brought other people, and possibly some of their friends, into your network.

You can also put links on to your blog page that you think people might find interesting. This adds another strand to your network and gets your link put on other people's sites and blogs – yet another strand.

brilliant tip

If you have a website as well as a blog, link them to one another. This will give you more presence in the 'eyes' of the search engines and make you easier to find.

Whatever you do, do not start a blog then not update it, as a blog that has not been updated for two months looks like a deserted town in the Wild West!

To get the best results from your blog think of it like a shop that you have to get people to come and look at, and all the pinging and the links as ways to attract people to take a look. With that in mind, do not forget to send an e-mail to your contacts telling them that you have updated your blog so that they keep coming back to look at it.

Be aware of the consequences of your blog and its accessibility to everyone, not just your selected audience. Increasingly, many employers are now checking blogs when researching the background of candidates. With any sharing technology, ensure that there is nothing that could compromise your employment prospects. If you blogged about how boring your job was and how you pretended to work all day while surfing the internet, you cannot be surprised if your employer takes a dim view of this.

> increasingly, many employers are now checking blogs

Setting up a blog

So how do you set up a blog? There are many sites that offer free blog space (see the appendix). Below is a guide to a free blog website to get you up and running.

- **Go to www.blogger.com**
- **Click where it says 'Create Your Blog Now'**.
- **Fill in a user name**. This can be anything you want – it is what you will use to sign in to your blog.
- **Select a password**. This must be at least six characters long. Try to use a combination of numbers and letters, and think of something that others will not be able to guess easily.
- **Select a display name**. This will be used to sign your blog posts, so choose something that will protect your identity! We recommend that you refrain from using your first and last name or, if you can be easily located with your first name, choose another name.
- **Enter an e-mail address**. You will need this to register, and later on you can change your preferences so this will not appear on your blog in clear sight of visitors.
- **Read the terms of service**, then click the box indicating you have done so.

- **Click 'Continue'.**

- **Give your blog a title.** This is what will show at the top of your blog page.

- **Choose a web address for your blog space.** This will display in the address bar as http://yourblogspacename. blogspot.com.

- **Choose a template.** Select from the templates the way you would like your blog to look. If you do not like anything you see then just select one to get started. We will show you how you can change or customise it later if you want.

brilliant tip

Consider setting up a separate e-mail account for your blog – this helps protect you from online predators.

Once your blog has been created, you are ready to change your personal profile and begin posting!

Posting to your blog

- Click on 'Start Posting' once your blog has been created.

- Create a title for your first posting and write your first post in the text box.

- Click 'Publish Post'. Publishing your post will make it live on your blog and visible on the Web.

- Each time you add a new post to your blog, you have to publish it before it goes up on the Web.

Microblogging

Microblogging is a popular form of blogging in which the entries or posts are limited to one or two short sentences or phrases, an image or an embedded video. The concise nature of this form of blogging makes the blogs very easy to maintain and very easy to follow, which accounts for the viral success that Twitter (http://twitter.com), the most famous microblogging website, has.

Twitter has over 100 million users (as at April 2010) and has established the term 'tweet' to describe the short posts (text) that are the essence of microblogging. These tweets are displayed on the author's profile page and can be viewed by users who subscribe to the author – known as 'followers'. This subscription aspect gives Twitter a social networking dimension.

brilliant tip

Register to send updates to Twitter from your mobile phone by text message.

 links

http://en.wikipedia.org/wiki/Blog

www.blogger.com

www.thoughts.com

http://twitter.com

Forums

Forums are very much like chat rooms where you can go to share opinions and ideas. Whereas the blog is somewhere to display your ideas and opinions, a forum is where you go to exchange them with other people.

Forums are either a site in their own right or exist as part of a website. Forums are very much run on a theme, for example, the Warrior forum specialises in wealth creation and personal development, and there are thousands of themed forums on just about every topic you can imagine.

> there are thousands of themed forums on just about every topic

You often find a forum within a website that allows customers of that website to exchange views and quite often resolve problems that they would otherwise have had to refer to the supplier. Sites selling technical products are a great example. Often the answer for the confused user is quickly supplied by another user through the forum.

Again, like blogs, by commenting regularly on forums and leaving your link you will find yourself being picked up by search engines and improve your rankings.

⤢)**brilliant** links

http://en.wikipedia.org/wiki/Internet_forum

Wikis

Wikis are websites that allows a group of people (e.g. families, clubs or organisations) total access to the site to review, change and add information. They are a great medium for networking as members from all over the country can access the site and add latest information to keep other members updated.

As with blogs and forums you can display links from other wikis on your site to grow your network even more.

↗ brilliant **links**

http://en.wikipedia.org/wiki/Wiki

www.wiki.org/wiki.cgi?WhatIsWiki

www.wikihow.com/Start-a-Wiki

MySpace

MySpace is currently the world's sixth most popular English language website so obviously a great place to network. It was set up as an international social networking website offering an interactive, user-submitted network of friends, personal profiles, blogs, groups, photos, music and videos.

This site has become incredibly popular very quickly, particularly with young people.

↗ brilliant **links**

http://en.wikipedia.org/wiki/MySpace

www.myspace.com

Netiquette

Netiquette is a term that has developed from internet etiquette or possibly network etiquette and is a guide for online behaviour, especially in chat rooms, message boards, forums and even e-mail. One obvious example is not posting in upper case, which is the online equivalent of shouting; another is refraining from commercial advertising outside a business-related online group. For a more comprehensive list of rules and guidelines, see the following links.

↗ **brilliant** links

http://en.wikipedia.org/wiki/Netiquette

http://tools.ietf.org/html/rfc1855

www.netmanners.com

Instant messaging software

Instant messaging (IM) is a form of communication that satisfies the functions of e-mail and phone. There are established brands like Windows Live Messenger, Yahoo Messenger, Skype and GoogleTalk, all of which allow people to connect easily with each other across varied geographical locations. Having a contact on instant messaging software is like having someone virtually sitting next to you whom you can talk to without having to pick up the phone. The beauty is that IM is less intrusive than a phone call. Of course, some IM software also allows you to have voice conversations, and if you both have a webcam you can even see each other as you speak.

> IM is less intrusive than a phone call

IM is a very powerful tool for managing your network, because communication acts as glue that binds your network closer to you. How well do you communicate with your network? How often? How strong is your network glue? Are you already using instant messaging software? If not, you must definitely add this to your networking toolbox. If you are already using it, here are some ways to get more out of it.

brilliant tips

- Organise your instant messaging contacts into relevant groups.
- Manage your status so that contacts know when you are available.
- Save and review key conversations to add more value to subsequent conversations.
- Respect your contacts' time and status – don't bug them if they're busy.
- Seek to make your conversations valuable for your contacts.

For a good overview of instant messaging and some useful links see the following links.

brilliant links

http://en.wikipedia.org/wiki/Instant_messaging

www.google.com/talk

www.skype.com

http://messenger.yahoo.com

http://explore.live.com

Electronic mailing lists

Electronic mailing lists are a method of extending a discussion to members without them having to log into a discussion forum. They simply reply by e-mail to the group and the conversation continues. It provides excellent networking opportunities. Three key examples are Yahoo! Groups, MSN Groups and Google Groups.

↗ **brilliant** links

http://en.wikipedia.org/wiki/Electronic_mailing_lists

http://groups.google.com

http://groups.yahoo.com

http://login.live.com

Chat rooms

Chat rooms are the online equivalent of meeting rooms where you can have conferences and meetings with people, both known and unknown to you. Technically, instant messaging and online forums could be considered a subset of chat rooms. Having already touched on those, we are now referring to the traditional online chat rooms like IRC (Internet Relay Chat), where people are not required to be invited (unlike with instant messaging). This provides a mechanism for meeting strangers without being physically present and is another way of growing your network.

> chat rooms are the online equivalent of meeting rooms

brilliant links

http://en.wikipedia.org/wiki/Chat_rooms

http://en.wikipedia.org/wiki/IRC

www.mirc.com/

www.paltalk.com

LinkedIn for business networking

There are many social networking websites, but for business or professional networking, LinkedIn stands out. Here is a true gem of a networking tool for career and business development! Whether you want to stay in contact with business partners and colleagues, find a job, hire people or ask for/show expertise, LinkedIn is a must.

LinkedIn has many features and benefits, but rather than reproducing the information here you should access the following links.

brilliant links

http://en.wikipedia.org/wiki/LinkedIn

www.linkedin.com

www.linkedin.com/static?key=tour_flash

www.rickupton.com/linkedin-tips.htm

www.linkedintelligence.com

Facebook

Facebook has been the big social networking phenomenon of the last few years and currently has 400 million users (as of 2010). These range from teenagers running their entire social lives on Facebook, to families and friends staying in touch and sharing experiences, to companies networking, to political and other campaigns. Facebook literally covers the full spectrum of social networking genres described in the TRACKER model.

brilliant tip

One key consideration with Facebook is protecting your privacy. Facebook provides many options and settings for this – use them.

Staying safe in the virtual community

Be good. But if you cannot be good, then at least be safe.

This piece of parental wisdom applies to all your online activities in the virtual community. The first part (be good) is to be sensible about where you go and who you interact with. The second part (be safe) is the underlying need to protect your privacy. More detailed advice on this is available at the following link.

brilliant link

www.wiredsafety.org

PART 4

Networking in practice

CHAPTER 13

Your business card

F irst things first: before you attempt to put networking into practice, you need to have a business card. A good business card is an essential means of exchanging accurate contact information elegantly, and ensures that if you meet someone you want to keep in contact with you have the means to do so. Business cards are a reflection of you and your 'brand', so it is essential you take some time to get the 'look' right.

brilliant tip

It is always handy to have a case to put your business cards in to protect them from getting tattered. Also have a pocket dedicated to storing business cards that you receive until you can file them. This way you will not have to go searching for them or accidently give someone else's card to a new contact instead of your own!

What makes a brilliant networking business card?

- The card must reflect your brand.
- It should be clean looking with information presented legibly.
- It must have your name, title, company and contact details clearly stated.
- It should make good use of space, so it is not cluttered.

- If it is in colour the colours should be compatible and selected tastefully.
- The card should be good quality and durable.

brilliant tip

If you are between jobs or job hunting, create a simple business card composed of your home contact details and your mobile number. This is far more professional than giving a card with your former company's details on it, or crossing out and writing on an outdated card.

What makes a poor business card?

- Too cluttered.
- Hard-to-read type.
- Poor quality card that creases or gets damaged easily.
- Poor colour scheme, making it hard to read.
- Does not reflect the image of the person or company.

brilliant tip

Have a mock up done of a business card. Ask friends or colleagues to give you feedback in terms of its legibility, look and feel. Ask what image it conveys and for any suggestions they have to improve the card.

Be selective with your card

Do not give out your card to all and sundry without care. Give it to people who ask for one or to anyone with whom you particularly want to stay in touch or whom you have spoken to.

These individuals might not be immediately relevant to you but in the future they could be your vital connectors.

do not give out your card to all and sundry

Sometimes it is obvious when cards should be exchanged. At some meetings they are exchanged at the beginning of the meeting, while at others at the end. In this case follow the cue and protocol. If cards have not been exchanged at the beginning and you do want to leave your card with people at the end, you can offer cards to them then.

brilliant tip

You can get business cards printed with blank lines on them. If the person you are making a request from does not have a card, offer them a blank card on which to write their details or offer them the back of one of your business cards to write their details on. If possible, never leave without the other person's details, especially if they are a client. Even if they have your details they might lose your card or never contact you. Remember to have a pen (that works!) on you. Paper without pen has been the cause of many lost contacts.

Using business cards in Asia

In Asia the business card is treated as symbolic – as a gift of identity by the giver to the recipient – and thus the protocol is very different to that in the West:

1   If you wish to exchange cards you offer the card with both hands and with the print up, showing consideration. This is also done with proximity, demonstrating intimacy between the parties.

2 Simultaneously you receive the other person's card, showing equality in the relationship.

3 When you have received the card, spend a moment reading it. This shows that you consider its content important. Take the time to make a positive comment on its quality or content. Again this shows attention as well as respect for the individual.

4 Do not put the card immediately into your pocket but leave it on display while you are still together so it is visible. This again shows respect and value for the person who is in your presence.

This can be contrasted to the way cards are exchanged in western Europe where they are hardly looked at and stuffed straight into a pocket!

CHAPTER 14

First
impressions

First impressions are crucial to your success as a networker. They are vital as they are often lasting impressions. Social psychologists say that we make decisions about people in the first few minutes, if not seconds, after meeting them. After this it is very hard to change our beliefs, as we unconsciously seek evidence to support them.

Even before verbal contact we have made a judgement that will inform how we interact with a person. The only concern is that our judgements might be wrong. An HSBC advert series called 'Your point of view' illustrates this perfectly. It shows a series of images seen from two different perspectives depending on your point of view. A face could be 'old' or it could be 'wise'; yellow could be 'bright' or it could be 'cowardice' depending on your cultural background or personal perspective.

Judging a book by its cover

To judge a book by its cover is really a basic description of first impressions. Another less comfortable word to describe this is 'prejudice'. Prejudice as a word is not necessarily negative, it simply means 'pre-judgement': to make a judgement in advance. Normally our prejudices are based again on past experience, memories and interactions, as

> our stereotypes are powerful and often unconscious

well as shaped by the media, our upbringing and culture. Our stereotypes are powerful and often unconscious.

What has this to do with networking? By making a pre-judgement and excluding individuals from the possibility of connection you are also excluding yourself from the opportunities and benefits that connecting to them might provide.

brilliant tip

Your first impression is your moment of choice, the chance to question your judgement and to connect to opportunity.

Organisations are realising that by failing to capitalise on a wide variety of staff with different perspectives, they are less able to be competitive. This is increasingly the case with short-ages of qualified staff and a global customer base. And just as an organisation might suffer from lack of diversity, equally this would apply to an individual. So you need to benefit from as wide a knowledge pool as possible.

brilliant tip

The best way to see if you have any unconscious prejudices is to look at your current network map. How diverse is it, based on the possibilities that are available to you in your situation? Are the people you network with all of the same gender, age bracket, race or creed? If this is the case see if you can identify ways to move beyond your normal network to widen your base. This might be achieved by attending community events, going to different places and making the effort to speak to people who are unlike yourself.

So, given that we are aware of who we connect with and the influence first impressions can have, what can we do to use this influence to network brilliantly?

How to create a brilliant first impression

According to the field of NLP (Neuro Linguistic Programming – see the appendix), impressions can be influenced by sensory factors. NLP breaks down impact into parts based on the predominant physical senses – the way others perceive us, through sight, sound and feeling (touch). This is encapsulated as:

- **V**isual – what you look like.
- **A**uditory – how you sound.
- **K**inaesthetic – the 'feeling' you create.

The key is to maximise these to achieve your full potential.

Visual

Dress well

Are you dressed appropriately for the event? If the event is advertised as 'black tie' this means that business suits are not an option. Different events will have different dress codes. The clothes you wear *will* send messages to those who look at you, so make them ones you want to communicate. If in doubt on dress code, it is better to dress 'up' rather than 'down'. For example, it is easier to take off a tie or jacket to look more informal than to find them at an event if you come in a T-shirt!

> it is better to dress 'up' rather than 'down'

brilliant tip

Often we know somebody who does dress well and we admire their style. Perhaps it is worth approaching them and asking their advice.

Check your badge

At networking events it is very common to be given a name badge. Check that your name and company have been spelt correctly and that if the badge is handwritten it is legible. Also important is to keep the badge visible. A good place to put the badge is on your right breast pocket or suit lapel. This is because the eye is naturally drawn there when shaking hands with someone.

Look your best

Grooming is essential. Make sure everything is neat, trimmed and you are looking and smelling your best. Although not a visual component, smelling good is an essential of grooming. With fragrances do not go over the top – less can be more. At one event I went to guests were so over-empowered by the strong aftershave of one presenter, even though he was excellent they kept well away from him throughout the day!

Sometimes we are told that wearing unusual items (e.g. a piece of jewellery or an interesting tie) can generate conversation. Although this is true, keep it to a minimum. The Bart Simpson tie your cousin got you for Christmas might lead to a discussion, but it might not convey the impression that you want to give. Have the item lead into a discussion that takes you down a route leading towards your goal: for example, a tie appropriate to a business school or topic you want to talk about.

Feel comfortable

Make sure that what you are wearing is comfortable as well as smart – especially if the event involves standing on your feet all evening. Do a mirror check before leaving home to make sure everything is in order.

brilliant tip

Smile!

The best thing you can wear visually is a smile. Smiles often attract people as they give the message you are friendly and approachable. This is far more successful than looking pristine but aloof and unfriendly.

Auditory

Use your *own* accent

How you sound has a marked impression on the way people perceive you. Just note the different stereotypes associated with different regional accents across the UK and the world. It is important not to fake an accent or be someone you are not. I heard a story of an Englishman who faked a Welsh accent when speaking to a Welshman and a Scottish accent when speaking to a Scot. Suddenly he found himself meeting them both together – of course he then switched into his own accent!

Talk clearly

One of the most common vocal mistakes made by poor communicators and networkers is that they talk too fast. This can often be because of nerves or being unclear about what they are going to say. In this case it is beneficial to practise breathing exercises and to remember to pause. Just dropping your shoulders and taking one deep breath can help you relax.

Be aware of the tone of your voice

Normally a deep, resonant voice commands authority while a high, shallow voice does not. While we are born with our own voices, there is a lot of work that can be done to improve the quality and tone of voice and this is well worth the investment. Many adult colleges offer courses in voice coaching at a fraction of the cost of one-to-one tuition.

With a growing proportion of people working flexibly from home, the phone has increasingly become a major communication tool. In this case your voice also replaces all the influence visual communication would have had.

Use words wisely

Often we perceive those with a greater vocabulary to have greater intelligence. Vocabulary is often used by psychologists as a measure of healthy child development. There is a big difference between using words that are so obtuse people need to look them up in a dictionary to using a wide variety of easily understood words to add interest. Unless you are with individuals who use slang, avoid it. Increasing your vocabulary and using words appropriately is a sure way to build credibility. Some of the interesting and relevant courses to take can be found from an online search, or you might choose to learn one new word a day and aim to use it in context. Over time the impact will be considerable.

> we perceive those with a greater vocabulary to have greater intelligence

Kinaesthetic

Know how you feel

There are many ways that we can influence how we come across to others and how we make them feel. Perhaps the most important one, but one which we are not often taught, is being aware of our own state – how we are feeling. Have you ever noticed that if you are around someone who is really nervous or agitated it is easy

> it is very easy to be influenced by the state of those around us

to become nervous and agitated too? The converse is also true – if you are around a cheerful and relaxed person it is easier for you to feel that way also. It is very easy to be influenced by the state of those around us, especially if they are experiencing strong emotions (e.g. anger or grief).

Change how you feel

One of the ways that you can create a feeling of relaxation is by changing your state.

The first step, when making a first impression, is to become aware of how you are feeling right at that moment. As you read this book what word(s) would you use to describe how you are feeling at this moment? For example, you might be **relaxed** or you may be **alert, tired** or **full of energy**. What word would you use to describe how you are feeling now? Take a few moments just to *be aware of how you feel*. Give it as accurate a label as you can.

Now that you have identified your state, imagine that you are **mildly sad** about something. It does not have to be a big thing but just think of something now that gives you that feeling. *Be the person you would be now if you are feeling mildly sad*. If you find it hard to think of something that you are mildly sad or upset about, then just pretend you are sad. Really take on the part. How would you be standing or sitting? How would you walk? Put this book down and do the exercise.

Did you notice that when you thought about the thing that made you mildly sad, your physiology (body posture) changed? You might have put your head down. Perhaps you had your shoulders drooped forward or tensed up. If you were walking perhaps you were walking slowly with your eyes on the floor. Just notice how in the exercise your state was reflected in your body.

brilliant tip

Your physiology is connected to your internal state. Once you know that your body is neurologically connected to display how you feel, you can start to alter your body language.

Now I want you to look upwards at a point in front of you that is a few feet above eye level. Then I want you to **say out loud** 'Yes! Yes! Yes!' again and again. (It is best to do this in an empty room so you are not observed!)

Now that you have done this you might notice that you find it difficult not to smile, or at the least you no longer have your sad feelings. Just by changing your physiology, your body stance, you can change your state, and your feelings change too.

It was very difficult, if not impossible, to remain sad while looking up and repeating these words constantly. Why? The answer is you were in a *parasympathetic state*. This state is created when a situation requires a fight or flight response. It is a heightened state of awareness in which you cannot experience any negative self-talk or emotion. (You know, the kind of talk that says 'I'm going to be too nervous to speak to

> in this state there is only room for action

strangers', 'I don't have the confidence', etc.) In this state there is only room for action.

Put it into practice

While networking at conferences or events it can sometimes be very easy to get bored and to lose concentration. In this case notice that when you get bored or lose concentration you adopt a certain posture. Perhaps in a large room you sit with your spine bent, feet up on the chair in front, and almost in a crouch-like position where you can hardly see or hear the speaker. Or perhaps in a one-to-one conversation you slouch and tend to look over the shoulder of the person talking rather than making eye contact.

If you want to concentrate, simply **change your posture** to reflect that you are alert and want to learn. If sitting, try sitting upright with your back straight. Keep your head up with your eyes looking at the speaker. Try it. Perhaps also sit slightly forward on the edge of your seat.

Just by changing your posture to be upright you will notice that you can now concentrate. Suddenly you no longer feel bored but are curious as to what the speaker has to say.

What is interesting is that your physiology not only affects your state but it also influences how you behave. For example, if you are feeling happy you will behave cheerfully, perhaps laugh a lot and be helpful, etc. If, on the other hand, you are feeling negative, or even angry, you might behave sharply with others, criticising or snapping for no reason. In turn, your behaviour will affect your results. If you behave cheerfully and do positive things it is likely that people will feel drawn to you. If you are angry and shout at others it is likely that they do not like to keep your company.

If you change your state by changing your physiology you will change your results! That means networking more confidently and drawing people to you.

brilliant tip

Be aware of your physiology when you walk into a room or when you meet people. Are you standing upright? Are your shoulders down and relaxed? Before you enter a room, if you are nervous notice how your body is and take a few moments to correct it before walking into the room.

Alpha state

Another way that you can affect kinaesthetically your networking performance is to put yourself into an *alpha state*. This is a relaxed state in which you are aware of what is happening around you. It is also known as the *learning state* or *peripheral vision*.

To do this, simply look up at a point on the wall or ceiling opposite a few feet above your eye level. If there is no wall or ceiling just find a spot to focus on that is straight ahead of you but a few feet above eye level.

Next, bring your awareness to the corners of the space in front of you, the furthest ends of what you can see ahead, while *keeping your eyes fixed ahead at the point above you*. It is important to not move your head or your eyes – just let your awareness expand and let your eyes relax. Be aware now of what is on either side of you, to the left and to the right, as well as in front, while still *keeping your eyes fixed straight ahead at the point above you*. Now imagine being aware of what is behind you, as well as what is to the sides and is in front, while still *keeping your eyes fixed straight ahead at the point above you*.

After a minute, bring your head and eyes down to your natural eye level, and begin networking while maintaining this relaxed state of awareness. If you practise going into peripheral vision you will soon be able to access it in a matter of a few seconds almost automatically. You will also notice many things around you that you would have missed. You will see patterns in the room and notice more about what is happening and how people are moving, even though you are not looking directly at them.

If this feels strange at first it is because from childhood we are used to *fovial vision* (tunnel vision), yet peripheral vision is the ideal networking state. Just practise this and notice how your results change and how much easier you find it to be aware of other people.

> from childhood we are used to *fovial vision* (tunnel vision)

brilliant tip

Just *before* entering a networking event or opportunity take a few moments to enter peripheral vision. Try to maintain this relaxed state of awareness as you speak to individuals so that you are looking at them with attention, but know what is happening around you so that if you need to bring someone into the conversation or leave to meet someone else you can do so with ease and grace.

CHAPTER 15

The art of conversation

Getting started

So you've dressed the part, assessed your goals, improved your posture – now you have to get started, one-to-one, and that means initiating conversation, often with strangers. There is no one right way to do this – what is essential is that you do it! People generally do not have to say anything funny, meaningful or profound to start up a conversation. It could be something as simple as, 'Have you got the time?' Many people who are in friendships or relationships cannot remember the first words they said to each other. What is important is the contact and the feelings behind the contact.

Do some research before the event

One of the most important things to enable you to have confidence in approaching people at an event is to do background research on them. If you have been given details of other attendees, make use of this essential information. If they have a business, look at their website; if they have written a book, it would be good if you could read all or part of it prior to the event. This background research will allow you to ask thoughtful questions from the outset and also to continue the conversation later. For example, 'Hi, I've been wanting to meet you. I really enjoyed your book. What inspired you to write it?'

Say something positive or neutral

Saying that the food is terrible might start a conversation, but it may become a conversation that descends quickly into finding everything wrong with a situation and you, by association, appearing as a complaining person. A far better method would be to ask something neutral like, 'Did you have far to come to get here today?' or 'Why did you decide to come to this event?', or to pay someone a genuine compliment.

Some subjects at networking events should be avoided unless you have come together to discuss them specifically. These include religion and politics, which can be highly emotive because of conflicting ideas, emotions or perceptions. A sense of humour is a bonus but jokes that are targeted at or offensive to individuals and groups should also be avoided.

> some subjects at networking events should be avoided

▶brilliant example

Start with something that connects you both

If you are at a party or a dinner you might ask of another guest, 'How do you know so and so?' or 'Do you know anyone else here tonight?' If it is a business conference you might say, 'Hi, we haven't met, my name's Steven. This is my first time at this conference. Did you come last year?' Alternatively you might refer to an element on the programme: 'Have you heard this speaker before?' or 'What did you think of the last speaker?' Look out and observe details around you that could provide opportunities to connect with others.

If you have arrived with another person, go solo

One of the main barriers to networking is that *we naturally prefer to speak to the people we know*. If you have come in a group or with a partner, separate and meet new people. Often it is easier for people to approach those who are alone rather than in couples. You can compare notes with your partner or group afterwards.

Introduce yourself

Start by introducing yourself with a warm smile and simple introduction: 'Hello, pleased to meet you, I'm Steven.'

> give the person time to think and to feel comfortable

Generally the person will respond with their name and then the conversation will flow (we will explore how to make it flow below). Give the person time to think and to feel comfortable speaking with you.

brilliant tip

When you start a conversation with strangers, remember that they might also be feeling nervous or apprehensive. By being the first to start a conversation, you are the one breaking the ice, and will be perceived as being confident. A simple question like 'I've just arrived and don't seem to know anyone here. Are you in the same boat?' can give the other person a chance to connect.

Names are there to be used

Our names, especially first names, are possibly the one consistent label that many of us identify with throughout our lives. Many people take pride in their name and take time to discover its meaning. Even in a large crowd with a lot of noise, if someone calls your name you are still likely to hear it.

When someone remembers and uses our name it makes us feel valued as a person. They have taken the time to remember it and this in turn makes us feel special. Those well trained in sales or customer service know that the sweetest sound the customer can hear is their name repeated to them and that this then builds rapport and puts people on closer terms.

When someone forgets our name it can make us feel that we were not important enough to be remembered. The implication is that 'You don't matter' or at worst it can seem like deliberate rudeness, 'Your name is not important'.

When you arrive at an event and are introduced to a group of people quickly, do not be shy at this point to stop the host and just check you have all the names correctly. 'Sorry, I missed that, it was so fast, can I check, your name is …?' Taking the time now to hear and remember the names properly will save a lot of guesswork in the future. It is also understood and forgivable when you have just met to clarify such information.

When you are first introduced to someone you can use their name as you answer, to reinforce it in your memory, for example:

'Hi, I'm Katie.'

'Hi Katie, good to meet you.'

Although it might sound awkward, you have a far better chance of remembering the name, saving embarrassment later.

Once you have a name, remember to use it occasionally during the conversation or as you are finishing the conversation. This will help reinforce it. If the person has a name badge or you have been given a business card, referring to these when you have quiet times at the event and associating them with the person's face will also help you remember.

If in doubt it is always better to ask for a name than to guess. Although this is clumsy it can be more easily forgiven than if you use the wrong name all evening. 'Sorry, as I was coming in I missed your first name, could you repeat it?' 'Sure, I'm Mike.'

brilliant tip

If a name is difficult to pronounce or long, ask the person to tell you how to say their name rather than guessing and coming up with something of your own creation. 'Paramahansa, that's a beautiful name, how do I pronounce that correctly?' Unusual names can also be great conversation starters: 'That's a beautiful name, what does it mean?'

If you are asked to introduce someone to another person but you do not know their name, this is a sticky situation. There are very few ways to get out of it but one is to step back and assume that they can introduce themselves: '*Please go ahead and introduce yourself to each other, I would really like you to meet.*' Once they have said their names, take a mental note and remember them.

Forget yourself

Once you have done what you can to prepare to connect with someone and make the impression you want to give, the best thing you can do paradoxically is to forget yourself, 'let go' and be immersed in the person you are speaking to while being aware of the needs of others around you.

How to approach a group of people

The dynamics of approaching a group of people are slightly different than one-to-one situations but only at the outset. It is quite common for groups to be a collection of people having one-to-one conversations with the person next to them, rather than one person speaking at a time.

- Groups form early, so arrive on time or early at an event before closed groups have formed. If you can start a one-to-one conversation with as many people as you can, then if they later join a group you have a 'go to' person to approach who is familiar to you.

- Usually at every formal networking event there is a host or organiser. If you know that you want to join a group, asking the host to introduce you will normally allow you to break the ice without the burden being on you.

- Keep a close eye out and look for opportunities to join a conversation by speaking to a pair or the person at the end of a group, if the group is fractured. Again the opener does not need to be memorable. It could be, 'Do you know the football results?' if there is a match on, or 'Do you have the time?' to someone at the end of the group.

- If the event host does any icebreakers – even if these are just a round-robin of introductions – take note of any details about people you want to talk to. If they are in a group and you have something specific to see them about, you could flag the request at that point and request to speak later. Always acknowledge that you are interrupting a conversation. For example, 'Excuse me, I don't want to disturb your conversation but in the introductions I heard that you work in the pharmaceutical industry. I'm a researcher. I know you are busy now but would it be possible to chat to you later this evening?' On many occasions the person will continue the conversation with you then and there.

- Sometimes the group could be at a conference or forum and you want to get noticed. One of the easiest ways to do this is to ask a short intelligent question if questions are taken after speakers. Being the first person to do this also illustrates confidence. You can phrase the question in such a way that people know who you are and what you do. For example: 'Claire Smith, novelist and copywriter. I really enjoyed the point you made about grammar schools. Do you believe that they support a meritocratic educational system?'

- Sometimes when people are in a pair or a larger group they will be open to outsiders and you can then join them on their invitation. Other groups might want to stay private and although they may be polite at first, essentially they do not want you to join. Listen and look out carefully for verbal and non-verbal cues and if you do not get a positive response move quickly and politely on. There will always be more people to speak to.

> if you do not get a positive response move quickly and politely on

Keeping the conversation going

The main skill here is not having a fantastic story to tell or even to be witty, instead the key to keeping conversations going is to **listen carefully and ask thoughtful questions**.

When an experiment was carried out that involved a control group meeting a range of people in sequence, some of the people asked a lot of questions while others virtually did all the talking. Each subject in the control group was asked to rate how interesting they thought each person they met was. The surprising result was that those who listened more and spoke less were consistently rated as being more interesting. **To be interesting, be interested**.

brilliant tip

When you are with someone, regardless of whether you are speaking or listening, one way to keep engaged is to hold a positive intention towards the other person. By this I mean to think about the person in a positive way. While I am not proposing that people are telepathic, sometimes our body language reflects our thoughts. When there is inconsistency between what you say and your body language then people do not believe your words. You will appear insincere.

The following ten points are worth bearing in mind.

1   Listen for key words or information and ask open questions based on the information appropriately. For example, if someone says they work at Faber Maunsell, it makes sense to ask them what their company does if you are not familiar with it. Sometimes details are dropped in incidentally: for example, 'Last week I dropped my son off at university which is near here, feels like I've done this journey a thousand times.' Here you have information to kick start a range of questions you could ask, about the university, about his son, about the course his son is taking, each of which could lead to further conversation.

2   There is a fine line between asking questions and interrogation so be aware of **sharing something about yourself** as appropriate and let the conversation flow between you. Try to link their stories to your own experience in some way but without dominating the conversation.

3   Be focused on your intent to share your aims for the conversation early. This might be asking plainly 'Why are you here?' or 'How did you decide to come to this conference?', and then sharing your main aims.

4   Start with closed questions. If you receive a positive
    response you can move on to ask more open questions that
    require more than a one-word answer. The quickest way to
    do this is to use one of the following to start your question:
    what, why, how, where, who or when? If the person you are
    speaking to is particularly shy or does not feel comfortable
    talking with people they do not know, then it makes sense to
    build the conversation gradually.

5   If you are in a group, ensure that you make eye contact
    with everyone and do not isolate any particular individual.
    This can happen sometimes unintentionally. A 20-minute
    reminiscence about old school days or how the office used
    to be might be fun, but probably not for the person who did
    not go to your school or work in your office. Check to see
    if everyone is engaged and bring in people you feel are not
    included. Normally this can be done in a subtle way, 'Mike,
    which school did you go to?' or 'Was it similar in your
    company?' This attention to the individual will let the group
    feel comfortable in expressing their opinions.

6   Another tip to keep conversation fresh in a group is to
    bring in other people who can add something or change the
    direction of the conversation. 'Hi, come and join us, we're
    just talking about...' can open the door to another person to
    connect with.

7   Summarise and paraphrase to show understanding. A
    useful tool to keep conversation going is to check your
    understanding of what the other person is saying. Not only
    does this keep you focused but done in the right way it
    demonstrates that you are listening. This can be done by asking
    a simple question and then repeating back in summary form
    what you have heard the person say. For example, 'Can I
    just check I understood that? You have been coming for five
    years and you have never been introduced to the chair of the
    conference' would be a neat summary.

> ### ✸ brilliant tip
>
> When you connect people or make an introduction be sure to say more than their names. Give them a hook or piece of information that will allow them to continue the conversation together: for example, 'Come and join us' is OK but 'Come and join us, I'd like to introduce you to Daniel who is here for the first time this evening and runs an internet company in Roehampton' is brilliant. When connecting two people you know, highlight any mutual interests that they might have.

8 Paraphrasing is using the near exact words somebody uses, and repeating them. Normally a few key words are enough. Using a similar example, a paraphrase of the statement would look as follows. Statement: 'I've been coming for five years but I've never been introduced to the chair of the conference.' Paraphrase: 'You've *never been introduced* to the chair of the conference?' To avoid the person feeling like you are parroting them, it is essential that you do not use the paraphrase too often. Done occasionally it is a powerful tool that lets others know you value their input.

9 The brilliant networker will also *listen out for the emotion or feeling behind the words* being said and check this out with the speaker. Emotion can be seen from body language, heard in the tone of voice or be evident in their facial expression. Networker: 'You've never been introduced to the chair of the conference. You seem upset by that. Am I right?' Person: 'Yes – I do feel angry that I've never been introduced.' Notice how the networker checked for understanding rather than simply saying 'You are upset', which may be an incorrect assumption. When reflecting back an emotion we are showing empathy with another. This is not the same as agreement or sympathy but gives the person the feeling that they are understood.

10 Remember that the person you are speaking to has needs
    and wants. Always listen with the intention: 'How can
    I assist this person?' and 'Who do I know that I could
    connect them to for advice or help?' Then offer to make the
    connection without pressure but as a genuine desire to help.

If you read around the subject of *emotional intelligence*, a term
first coined by Daniel Goleman, you will see how important
the emotions are for making
decisions even if we know
logically we should take
another course of action.
Brilliant networkers are able
to build strong emotional

> brilliant networkers are
> able to build strong
> emotional links

links with those they speak to, creating the foundations for
future relationships.

Be 'appropriately vulnerable'

One of the most powerful ways that you can keep a conversation going is by showing *appropriate vulnerability* – sharing your
feelings. For example, 'I'm feeling a little nervous. This is
my first time at a networking event and I don't seem to know
anyone.' By expressing our vulnerability we express our human-
ness and make it easier for people to relate to us. Often they
might be experiencing the same feelings as we are and by voic-
ing them we give others permission to do so too.

Be curious!

Brilliant networkers are generally curious people. While some
are experts in their field they often have a wide range of interests and friends, and are well read. This enables them to start
and maintain conversations on a wide range of topics. As mentioned at the beginning of the last chapter, brilliant networkers
know the value of diversity, which opens them up to a wider
range of opportunities. Think of the process as a Scrabble

board and the letters as types of contacts. You would never win the game by only using multiples of the same letter. The wider the variety of contacts you have, the more combinations available, the higher your chance of success.

brilliant tip

Next time you go to the newsagents pick up a magazine about a subject that you know nothing about and flick through it. Broadening our horizons and knowing what is happening in the media and around the world opens up paths of conversation that otherwise would have remained closed. Read your industry publications as well as a quality broadsheet and tabloid so you have a spectrum of views.

How to end a conversation

Even though we might enjoy a conversation, at some point it is obvious that both parties have run out of interesting things to say and the conversation has lost its purpose. Below are some ideas for ending a conversation gracefully.

Connect them to someone else

Rather than abruptly leaving a person standing or sitting, which is plain rude, one of the best ways to leave a conversation is to connect the person to someone else in the room by making an introduction. This might mean saying, for example, 'Paul, I would like to introduce you to Niall who is an accountant. Niall, this is Paul who is a lawyer for Global Bank.'

Once the introduction is made, you step out and walk away. Done naturally this gives a good chance for you to meet someone else and also for the person you left to make a new connection with somebody they just might have more in common with or gain information that could be of benefit.

Give a plausible reason to leave

For example: 'I'm really sorry, I've enjoyed our conversation, but I need to check whether my friend has arrived. It was great speaking to you and I hope you enjoy the evening.' Or 'I'm really sorry but I must go because I need to speak to Jack before he leaves. It was great speaking to you. Can I introduce you to our sales manager before I go?'

brilliant tip

Apply the five-minute rule. Five minutes is generally long enough to start a conversation and to ask questions to find mutual interests. If there are no obvious synergies, thank the person you are speaking to and exchange contact details. **Never leave the person alone** but again introduce them to someone whom you have met earlier who you think would be a useful connection or look to bring someone else into the conversation. You never know when someone can help you. Later on down the line that person could be the one individual you most need to know. Always be respectful and mindful, and don't forget to exchange contact details.

Finally, before you leave any event make sure that you have said goodbye and thanked the host. Often the host will be circulating but it is vital feedback and appreciation which will lead to more invitations. Double check that you have met everyone you wanted to and then leave. If you are done, avoid hanging around or lingering until the very end. Not only is this an inefficient use of your time but the hosts might be wanting people to leave so they can wrap up the event and clear the venue.

Ask for what you want

The reason you are networking is to accomplish your goals and so no matter how well a conversation is going it is important that you ask for what you want. Asking for what you want is powerful but it also needs to be done in such a way that it will give you the information you need.

> it is important that you ask for what you want

In their book *The Power of Networking* (1999), Sandy Villas and Donna Fisher suggest using the question 'Who do you know who...?' rather than 'Do you know anyone who ...?' to make a request. The latter can be answered with a closed yes or no, ending further conversation. By asking the former question the person is forced to think of people they know.

Some other powerful networking questions that Villas and Fisher highlight are:

- *'Who do you know who I should know (given the following circumstances)...?'*
- *'Who do you know who knows...?'*
- *'Who do you know who would benefit from...?'*
- *'Who would you recommend I contact about...?'*
- *'I am looking for... Who do you know who...?'*
- *'I would like to know the names of people you know who...?*

Asking the right questions opens up new possibilities to further your networking goals.

Share your goals early

As a general rule, when time is short at an event, it is important to share your goals early. You might enjoy the company of the person and want to spend more time with them on a future occasion, but it is important that you try to meet as many people as possible – without being rude and without spoiling the event for yourself.

You need to strike a balance. Networking should be as enjoyable and fun as meeting new friends, not a stressful race akin to a non-stop, one-day tour of several capital cities in the world. This is where the value of knowing in advance who is going to be at an event allows you to focus your attention. Be open to serendipity and to all you meet. It could be the person in the lunch queue who introduces you to your future partner. The key is to be open and ready to connect to everyone.

The hard sell

Perhaps one of the main reasons that networking has a bad name is because of individuals who approach you like pit-bull terriers, promoting their products shamelessly and not letting you go until you have either signed up or promised to let them contact you with further information.

When you approach someone at a networking event – although it is important to be clear about what you do and can offer – the aim is to develop a long-term relationship, not simply make a quick sale. When networking, ensure you are making requests, not demands.

Networking requests

Demanding	'I need you to give me...'
Empowering	'I am looking for... and thought you might...'
Vague	'I would like to contact good prospects for my business.'
Clear	'My ideal client is... Who do you know who...?'
Manipulative	'If you will... I will...'
Empowering	'I have some people to refer to you who... and keep me in mind when you meet people who...'
Hesitant	'I know you're busy and probably won't have time and I don't want to bother you, but...'
Straightforward	'I would like your assistance, if possible. Any amount of time you can give me will be appreciated.'
Too broad	'I am looking for a job. Who can you recommend that I talk to?'
Specific	'I am looking for job with a... company that can use my ... expertise. Who do you know who...?'
Confusing	'Do you think you could help me sell some of my widgets to people who have gadgets?'
Clear	'I want to contact people who are looking for widgets to better... Who do you know who I could call?'

From *The Power of Networking* (1999) by Sandy Villas and Donna Fisher, Thorsons.

brilliant tip

Before making a request take a moment to think about what you really need and refine your request so that it meets the criteria in the box opposite. Think about how you can also assist the other person with a need they might have.

CHAPTER 16

Handling rejection

Perhaps the most powerful force in shaping human behaviour is the fear of rejection. The fear of 'No', 'Go away', 'Who do you think you are?' or something a lot less amiable – the fear of being snubbed. We all experience this in one way or another and it hurts so much because we all have the need to belong. This is perhaps one of the core fundamental needs that make us human and enable us to live in society.

Often this fear of rejection prevents us from networking. If we learn to control and manage this fear then we can network more effectively and successfully.

> fear of rejection prevents us from networking

'No' just means 'no'

Often because of our experience we interpret the word 'no' in a very negative way. To us 'no' can mean 'No – you're not good enough' or 'No – I don't like you'. Recognise that 'no' simply means one thing, 'no', and the rest that we have added around it is our interpretation, which might or might not be true. Next time you hear the word 'no' listen to your thoughts. What are you making the word mean? You might want to challenge your thoughts by asking 'Is it true?' or 'Can I be absolutely 100 per cent sure that their "no" means this?'

Every 'no' brings me closer to a 'yes'

So the saying goes. What this means is that every time you hear someone say 'no' it does not necessarily mean that you have to give up instantly. The person who you might be making the request to may be having a bad day and if you ask them again later in the day, or perhaps next week, they might give a different response. The secret is either to ask again or to ask someone else.

Be flexible

Perhaps the masters at dealing with rejection and still getting their way are children. Which couple has not experienced the following when shopping:

Child: 'Dad, please can I have some sweets?'

Dad: 'No, it's before your dinner.'

Child: 'Please, I will eat all my dinner.' Tugging dad on the trouser leg.

Dad: 'No, it will spoil your appetite.'

Child: 'Dad, that's not fair, Mum would buy me sweets.' Scowling and banging feet.

Dad: 'No she wouldn't.'

Child: 'You just don't love me.' Now crying.

Dad: 'Yes I do, you just can't have sweets now.'

Child: 'No you don't.' Now bawling and screaming.

Dad: 'OK, I will buy some. Stop crying. You have to have them after dinner though.'

Child: 'OK.' Whimpering (but recovering!).

In this example, who showed the most flexibility? It was the child. When they discovered that their request was not working they tried a different approach, then another – then another until dad gave in!

This is not to say you should stamp your feet if you are rejected, but think about how you could approach the same problem but in a different way. Could you think of a way of genuinely meeting the needs of the other person or creating positive value for them to collaborate? The main thing is that a different

> the main thing is that a different strategy is used

strategy is used. You can also ask for feedback from the person, why they denied your request, or think about how you could reflect on the experience. A good question to ask yourself is: '*How could I have done this differently and more effectively?*' or '*In what other ways would this be possible?*'

Get over it!

Life is such that we will not always get what we want all the time. Although you can make an honest request from someone it would be manipulative at best and narcissistic at worst always to expect to get your own way. Sometimes the most respectful (to yourself) and appropriate thing you can do is to walk away from rejection knowing it might say more about the other person than about you.

Carole Stone, author of books on networking, gives her response to snubs. She says:

If you know the person well, simply ask, 'Did you really mean to be that rude?' Otherwise forget the snub, you'll be over it in a couple of hours.

CHAPTER 17

The elevator pitch

Often at some events, especially speed networking events, there is an opportunity to make a short presentation on your product or your reason for being there. In networking terms this is known as the elevator pitch – a description of what you do in 30 seconds or less, about the time it takes for the elevator to reach ground level.

How to make a brilliant pitch

1 Remember the power of first impressions. How you come across will have as much impact or even more impact than the words you say.

2 Allow time beforehand to prepare yourself and get into a positive state of mind.

3 When introducing yourself do not use jargon or technical language without explaining it simply. Try to describe your job in a way that engages interest rather than puts people to sleep. Never use titles that are unfamiliar to anyone (e.g. 'I'm an SEO, Grade 7').

4 It is essential you establish your credibility before people really listen to you. This is particularly the case in organisations that value status. To do this you can either put your title in the introduction (e.g. 'Director' or 'Manager') or if you are too junior you can stress the benefits and credibility of the company (e.g. 'I work for Global Bank,

one of the top-tier banking companies in the world'). If you are self-employed you might call yourself the founder of your company. If it is a small business you might describe its importance to the community. If you have won any awards, mention them in your opening line.

5   Keep to the point. One of the ways to do this is to think of the three most important points you want to get across and to have a sentence example for each one. These points are then topped and tailed by your main message.

6   When presenting your pitch, unless absolutely essential there should be no need for PowerPoint. Too many speakers rely on PowerPoint but slides tend to distract the listener from you and unless impressive will not be supportive of your point.

7   Make eye contact and smile. Even if your message is positive, if you appear aloof and distant you are unlikely to build rapport with the audience. Ensure you look around at all of the audience and not only to one group or side of the room. You might have to do this consciously at first, but with practice you will feel more comfortable and at ease.

8   On a practical level, ensure that you project your voice so that you can be heard by everyone, especially if the hall or event place is large. The worst thing is doing a great pitch and nobody hearing you. If you want more advice on delivering presentations it is well worth investing in a course at a local college that will improve your presenting skills. Also there are organisations such as Toastmasters (listed in the appendix) that give you opportunities to develop your public speaking skills further.

> the worst thing is doing a great pitch and nobody hearing you

9   Use handouts at the end. Avoid giving out any material before you speak as this will distract your listeners.

Distributing handouts after speaking reinforces the message and makes it far more likely that listeners will remember your main points.

10 Tell people what you want them to do as a result of your communication. They should not be left guessing as to what is required or what you can provide. This is sometimes termed a 'call for action'.

11 Ensure you thank people for listening to you so attentively.

12 Practise your elevator pitch in front of the mirror or to a friend. Ask for feedback as to clarity, pace and whether they understood what you do and what you want.

The box summarises the process.

Name, Business and Credentials

Main message

Point 1 – example

Point 2 – example

Point 3 – example

Main message repeated

Call to action and thanks

▶ brilliant example

Hello, I'm Steven, author of a book called *Brilliant networking* and also author of the bestselling book *Made in Britain* published by Pearson Education, who also own Penguin and the FT.

My main message is that **networking is essential for career success**.

Networking produces contacts, who can be influential for information on positions that occur. More than 60 per cent of people get their jobs informally through who they know – these jobs are never advertised.

Networking allows you to raise your profile, so that people know what opportunities you are looking for. This makes it more likely that opportunities will find you.

Lastly, networking can be fun, enabling you to develop a strong network and friends at work. These will support you when you need that extra hand and will keep you going through the tough times we all experience now and again.

In short, networking is the essential skill for career success.

I have copies of my book *Brilliant networking* here today. In it I share many of the secrets of brilliant networkers. Books are available for sale at a discount. Thank you for listening.

The above could be made even more effective if I tailored it to the audience I am addressing. For example, if I was speaking to a group of small businesses my main point should be 'networking is essential to the growth of small businesses' and then my three points should illustrate why. Remember people have short attention spans. You need to speak to their interests directly and answer their question: 'What's in it for me?' Be clear as to why they should be listening to you.

brilliant tip

A secret that many public speakers use when speaking to groups is to choose one person to make eye contact with initially. It helps if this person is about three-quarters of the way down the room and in the centre. The speaker then imagines they are having a one-to-one conversation with this person.

After a few moments the speaker smoothly changes direction and looks at another part of the room, connecting with another individual. This is repeated throughout the speech.

The benefit of this technique is that it allays the speaker's nerves. They feel they are having a relaxed one-on-one conversation. More importantly, even though you are speaking to one individual the audience feels you are connecting to them as a whole.

PART 5

Managing your network

CHAPTER 18

Follow-up

S o you have met the person and have the business card, now what? One of the most common mistakes of networkers is to go along to events and collect business cards that now gather dust. You come upon them weeks later and cannot even remember the person who gave it to you or why you would have it. Rather than throw it away you keep it, in case it is important, while more cards add to the pile.

Does the above sound familiar?

The art of follow-up

Immediately after the event at which you have received the business card, or when you reach home, take a few moments to record the following on the back of the card:

- Where you met the person and when.
- What was your purpose in exchanging the cards (e.g. 'promised to contact if I was ever in New Zealand' or 'a great copywriter').
- The day you met and any other interesting facts about the person (e.g. they like cricket and have two daughters at university).

The purpose of the above is to engrain in your memory details about the contact that might be forgotten if not recorded. Just summarise with a few bullet points what you felt was important in your conversation. For example, the points below could be noted immediately on the back of a business card while they are still fresh in your memory.

> ● Met at Sally's party 22/11/10.
>
> ● Send article on speed networking by 27/11/10.
>
> ● Loves hiking and water sports.
>
> ● Moving to London in 2011.

brilliant tip

Listen carefully during the conversation for points of interest that are meaningful to the person you are speaking to but that might not be directly related to their work. This could be their love of a sport or the fact they are planning to go on holiday to an exotic location next year. By noting these details it makes follow-up a lot more personal – and with impact.

Also note the following points:

● If you did not get a card, make sure that you write down the details you remember of the conversation immediately after the event. You could carry a small notebook for this purpose rather than fishing for scraps of paper or trying to write on the back of a till receipt.

● If you did not manage to get contact details for the person on the evening, the day after the event send an e-mail to the host asking for the person's contact details, thanking the host for a wonderful event and saying what a great connection you made. If the host is unwilling to give you these details, offer to give the host your contact details to pass on to the person you want to contact. The key here is not to give up.

● Sometimes you may have no luck getting contact details via the host. In this case start your search for contacts through what you know about each person. For example, if you know the individual works at *The Guardian* go on to the company website and see if you can locate the person online. Alternatively you might look at how the e-mails are structured in the company and send one in the same format (e.g. First name.Surname@company.com).

Have a system for recording your contacts

Once you have recorded the details it is essential that you collate them from the cards in a system that allows you to organise and retrieve information as and when needed. It really pays to make it a habit to do this the day you receive a card, ideally within 24 hours. Too easily one then becomes two and before you realise it more time has passed. There are various database options available but consider the following.

> make it a habit to do this the day you receive a card

Outlook or equivalent

Using an electronic system to store information is practical as most systems can be integrated into what you use for work, eliminating the need to have several databases when you need to find a contact. The advantage of Outlook is that you can easily share information by sending contact cards, and other people in your network will probably know how to use the system and have compatible software. The danger is that, unless you have a back-up, if something happens to your account or your PC you might lose all your contacts. Also if you do not have remote access to your contacts or a hand-held device the contacts are stuck in your PC when you might need them most.

Rolodex

Using a Rolodex has an advantage in that there is no risk of you losing contacts due to technology failure. Another advantage is that it is easy to look people up as you set the reference structure – whether as alphabetical, by business grouping or calendar month you met them. The disadvantage is that as the network grows – and I know some people who have 30,000 people in their networks – the Rolodex is no longer practical. Also searches are not easy to do when the numbers become very large or when you want instant information. In summary, for smaller networks, when there is a lack of access to technology, the Rolodex is fast and efficient.

Creating your own database

Making your own database on Excel, Access or other database software is highly recommended. It might be a simple table that captures what you want to know. The categories could be, for example:

- Name
- Date met
- Event
- Conversation
- Follow-up promised
- Last communication
- Connected to (here you can record if they are connected to people you want to meet, any specific groups and to other people in your network)
- Other notes.

brilliant tip

In 'Other notes' record key dates that are relevant to the person in a way you can access easily (e.g. birthdays, anniversaries, exam date, wedding of their son/daughter). Find out what is important to your contact over time and be sure to connect and send them best wishes on these occasions. Remember networking is about building a long-term relationship, not a one-off sale. By being attentive you demonstrate that the relationship matters.

By collating this information you really have a record of your relationship with a person. If they were ever to call and you have access to your database you would be able to give them specifics, or if you had to contact them again you would have the data at hand within a matter of seconds.

Online networks

As explored in Chapter 12 there are many online networking systems. The advantage of storing your contacts in these systems is that they are web-based so you can access them from any connected PC in the world. The disadvantage is that unless you have contact to the Web, the details

> it makes sense to be part of online networks but to have your main contact database separate

are unavailable to you! Also you rely on the network remaining popular so people continue to connect with you. With the pace of change in social networking technology it makes sense to be part of online networks but to have your main contact database separate, minimising your risk to changes in an online provider.

brilliant tip

Whichever system you choose to store your information on, remember that old information is useless information. Today people move jobs, change mobiles, e-mails or home addresses, and relocate abroad so it's essential that you check for updates periodically. You can do this each time you reconnect, as described in the following section, or you might choose to do this periodically (e.g. twice a year). In any case ensure you plan a method to keep your data fresh.

How to follow up

Nishma Gosrani from PricewaterhouseCoopers sent me the following on how she follows up on business cards:

I will write an e-mail (basics of e-mail is now a template) to them within 24 hours of meeting them, attaching a synopsis/profile and photograph of myself, also referring to the event that I met them at in the e-mail. I then usually follow this up over a drink, coffee, or sometimes even lunch. I have found that when I later meet people they remember me more often than other colleagues who they have met at the same event. I often follow this up by sending people on my list of contacts a greetings card to ensure that they have me/my company at the forefront of their minds should a business opportunity arise.

By e-mail

When following up by e-mail remind the person where you met, and provide some context to the follow-up. It could be simply to say that it was a pleasure to meet them and to thank them for their time.

When following up with several contacts you met at an event, never use the CC facility and copy everyone in. For a start they might not want their details shared with everybody and secondly it shows a lack of consideration and personal attention. A far better method is to write a generic e-mail that seems to be personally addressed and to put other contacts in the BCC facility.

▶ **brilliant** example

Hello

It was great to meet you at the Gold Convention last night. If you need any further information about the reports I mentioned please feel free to contact me. Attached is a sample. I wish you the best with your relocation and hope to meet you again at a future event.

Kind regards

David

Remember that e-mail exchange is not the most dynamic or appropriate way to build trust or develop a business relationship. Depending on your time and location, arranging to meet for coffee or for lunch could be much more profitable in taking things forward.

brilliant tip

Don't underestimate the value of a follow-up e-mail thanking people for their time. It illustrates not only respect but also continuity and will ensure you are remembered at a future date.

By phone

If following up by phone and you get through to an answer-phone, leave a clear message with your name, time of call, contact and when they can best reach you. Leaving a time to call avoids phone tag, which can be frustrating and provides a block to re-establishing connection.

> leaving a time to call avoids phone tag

Reconnecting

A great way to reconnect is to send information that you think the other person would find valuable based on your previous conversation. This need not be a big thing. It might be an article that you think they might like to read or an advert for a conference that might interest them. The key to this is to send it simply with a short message, asking nothing in return. 'Hope all is well. I thought this might interest you' will suffice. Sometimes this can lead to future business opportunities. Hemal Radia, a manifestation coach, sent me the following story about someone he met at a conference several years ago. By keeping in touch occasionally this later led to a business relationship.

I met Brad (his business partner) at a seminar in the mid-nineties. Just by saying hello and staying in touch for a few years this later led to countless adventures. We have worked on projects with multinational organisations in the UK and worldwide, coaching them and facilitating their sharing of knowledge and information, and in the process creating innovative and groundbreaking coaching and multimedia learning.

Connect them to others

A vital way to follow up is by connecting the person to other members of your network whom you think it would be valuable to meet. We explored this briefly in Part 3. Be generous with your contacts, but without giving too many of the details (e.g. an e-mail address might suffice). If unsure, check with your contact first that they are happy for their details to be shared. Remember that generosity with contacts often begets generosity.

brilliant **tip**

Always look to see how you can assist your network and offer help. If you only contact people when you need something this will be seen as always withdrawing from your emotional bank account with them – as highlighted earlier. Give regularly when you don't need anything.

Send brochures and newsletters

A convenient way to follow up with someone is by sending a free copy of your company brochure or e-newsletter. If you do not have one they are easy to create or you can get a professional to design a template for you which you can update by yourself (see the appendix).

If you are sending a physical brochure or printed material consider accompanying it with a hand-written personal message, numbers permitting. This personal touch again conveys the message that the person is important enough for you to take the time to write personally.

Sometimes you may re-establish contact but the person may not respond to you. As a general rule send no more than two reminders over a period of a few weeks to check if they received your communication. Sometimes e-mail and contact details change, so check these are still current.

If you still do not hear from someone it might be that they do not want to reconnect with you or that they do but it is not seen as a priority. The worst damage you can do is to contact them too frequently as it might offend or annoy them. Wait and send them an e-mail six months down the line – their situation might be different and then they may want to reconnect.

brilliant tip

If someone doesn't reply, never send an angry or discourteous e-mail. The chances are that you could meet this person again and there may have been good reasons why they did not reply, which are not personal to you. Instead, send an e-mail saying you are sorry they have not been in contact and that if they ever should need you to feel free to contact you at any time. You might drop them an e-mail again later in the year out of courtesy.

Avoid network fatigue

Once you have identified the forums available to you for networking face-to-face, it makes sense to record them in a way that you can compare and contrast the results, without creating network fatigue. This allows you to benchmark whether you feel the event gave value in terms of your time. You could create a simple table like the one below to monitor the effectiveness of all your networks, both face-to-face and online.

Networking group	Cost	Number of people	Times I attended	Sales generated	Maintenance (time spent)	Other benefits
Chamber of Commerce						
LinkedIn						
Business Link						

From the table you should be able to identify which networks are worth continuing with and which you should leave and cut your losses. Like gym memberships that are not used, being a member might be good in theory but in practice you could be wasting a lot of money and time. Review the benefits of attendance against your business objectives or the goals that you created for networking earlier.

brilliant tip

Track all your networks and memberships and review at least bi-annually. If you are finding that networks are taking too much time and money with little return you need to discontinue your membership. Be ruthless, as the time and money you save can be re-invested in more beneficial activities.

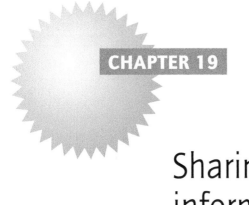

CHAPTER 19

Sharing
information

E-newsletters, whether monthly or quarterly, are also a low-cost way to share information with your network. The trick is to make them effective and manageable or you might spend more time writing them than doing business.

Creating effective e-newsletters

- **Keep them short and to the point**. Generally people do not read on screen as they would printed matter so it is important to provide information in 'bite-sized' chunks. You can do this by using multiple headers, bullets, short paragraphs and sentences, and links to further information. If you want to draw attention to longer documents, provide a brief summary of the document or its first few lines with a link to the full version on your website.

- **Don't block up inboxes** by sending e-newsletter files that are so big they clog up people's systems! It is best to keep e-mail messages under 100KB and do not send bulky attachments, like video or audio files. The recipient will just delete them in frustration. Instead, link back to that material on your website.

- **Be client focused** by providing information that is useful and relevant to clients. They will want substance, not press releases or promotional material, unless they have specifically agreed to receive advertising. If not, and it simply looks like a commercial, they will hit delete, and probably not read your future e-mails, even if these are not self-promotional. Focus on issues that affect your customers. Which past or future activities will they be interested in knowing about? What services do they need to know about that you now provide? You might choose to focus on a different topic or theme for each issue depending on the scope of your business and your network's interests.

● **Link to your website or blog**. An e-newsletter is a wonderful tool to draw people to your website or blog by using links. Your website can provide more detailed information about the stories in your e-newsletter, and it can also draw attention to other items of interest. The information on the website could provide links to related information such as press releases, other products, articles, etc. By providing readers with more information about the things that interest them you develop relationships as they also learn about the subjects that interest you.

● **Grab readers' attention from the beginning**. Many people are overloaded with e-mails – spam or otherwise. Unless the subject header compels the readers to open your e-newsletter the chances are they will never access it.

brilliant tip

Craft your subject line very carefully, since it is the first – and often the only – thing the reader will see. Put the most interesting and relevant information at the top, where it can also be seen if readers use a preview window to check e-mails.

● **Present your newsletter in HTML format** which, like a web page, can include colour and graphics that get people's attention. If you are having someone design your website look at the possibility of them designing an HTML template for your newsletters that gives a consistent feel to your website. Remember that even though you are using different media, branding should be consistent.

- **Don't send old news**. Is your material timely and relevant? In order to be of interest it should provide fresh information about topics on people's minds. Tips to do this include providing analysis on industry events or news that month,

  keep the material fresh and contemporary

  people's views on different subjects and also links to relevant web resources. Keep the material fresh and contemporary.

- **Interact**. Give readers the opportunity to do something. Readers who sign up for your newsletter probably have an interest in your subject and want to take part in sharing their opinions. Ask for feedback, stories and any opportunity to interact. Featuring readers' feedback or letters in each issue of the newsletter is also a good way to demonstrate that it is a debating forum for a community. This shows the e-newsletter is more of a dialogue, not a diatribe.

- **Take no prisoners**. Make it easy to subscribe and unsubscribe. All e-newsletters should have a simple link or button that allows users to be added or removed from the distribution list. Making it difficult to unsubscribe does not help your reputation and would be construed as invading privacy, or spamming if the person has requested not to receive it.

- **Give them everything**. Provide an e-newsletter archive on your website. This enables readers to refer back to past articles and demonstrates that you have a track record in providing quality and useful information. It also allows for a body of knowledge to be built on your website which you can look back on to chart progress or see themes evolving.

- **Respect privacy**. Have a clear, visible privacy policy and stick to it. You should be clear that you will not use personal information provided for any other purposes than to receive the e-newsletter and that the details will not be lent or sold to third parties. If you do intend to send mailings from partners you need to make this clear from the outset and provide an opportunity to opt out. This establishes trust and confidence essential to continuing the relationship.

E-brochures

All the rules above apply equally to e-brochures as to e-newsletters. Some additional pointers include the following:

- Ensure that you include a reader for your e-brochure's format. If you are sending a PDF, attach a link to a PDF reader that can be downloaded free to read your brochure.

- E-brochures tend to be one-off rather than regular e-newsletters. Still ensure that they are up to date and reflect your branding. They should be easy to read, crisp, clear and not cluttered. The e-brochure can also have a link to subscribe to your newsletter.

- Remember the e-brochure is essentially a sales brochure. Ensure that it has a fuller version of your elevator pitch, that it has a clear call to action and displays your contact details prominently. Testimonials from past clients are also very valuable.

- Some people dislike reading material on screen. Ensure that the e-brochure can be printed easily and when it is printed the format is not changed. State on the accompanying e-mail to the e-brochure that a hard copy can be provided if requested.

- Once you have sent your e-brochure, if you have a contact telephone number call to check that it has been received. Sometimes e-mail systems filter messages into a bulk folder. A one-time courtesy call will look professional but it should then be left to the recipient to contact you further if they wish.

Increasing distribution

Once you have an e-newsletter or an e-brochure, use this to build your distribution list and grow your network. As you develop the quality of your e-newsletter or e-brochure you will want to increase its distribution. This should not mean more development work for you but it will certainly mean more possible sales and a growth of your network.

- **Ask only for an e-mail address on your website**. People hate filling in long lists and if you are only sending them your newsletter you can limit the information you require to just an e-mail. The negative side is that this does not allow you to send targeted e-mails as you know nothing else about the customer, but there are other ways to build your main database. The purpose of the e-newsletter is permission to communicate with as many people as possible and to make it very easy for them to sign up.

- **Make it easy and obvious to subscribe**. By placing a one-click subscribe box at the same location on every page of your website you make it more likely that people will sign up.

- **Ask prospective clients if they want a copy of your e-newsletter**. If presented as a free item of value the answer will usually be yes but make sure you let them know that it is easy to unsubscribe so they do not feel obliged to continue.

- **Offer a free report in exchange for the e-mail address**. This could be in the format of 'Ten Top Tips for Publishing your Book', for example. The tips you send should be comprehensive but also lead to encouraging the reader to find out more information. For example: 'I hope you have enjoyed these top ten tips. For more free newsletters packed with useful advice click here (link to your newsletter).'

- **Speak up**. When speaking at events (perhaps at networking events) let those around you know at the end of your pitch that if they want any further information, free articles, etc. they can sign up for your newsletter at (web address). Consider using a line at the bottom of every e-mail that links to your free e-newsletter.

● **Explore teleclasses**. A recent offering is free teleclasses where people can telephone in and discuss a topic related to your subject. These can be advertised on your newsletter and normally last for one hour, perhaps once a month. Again this is a way to build a community. The cheapest providers of these services are often US teleconferencing companies. The service enables people to call in from anywhere in the world but at a low-cost, local call rate. Often the call is recorded and is available to listen to after the event, at the same number, for a limited time period.

● **Collect e-mail addresses at events**. If you are speaking at an event it is a good idea to have a clipboard in a prominent place or have a member of your team collect e-mail addresses from those who want to sign up for free services. You might choose to collect e-mails from business cards entered into a prize draw, but make it clear that participants will be signed up for the free e-newsletter – although they can sign out at any time.

> you might choose to collect e-mails from business cards entered into a prize draw

● **Encourage flow**. Encourage readers to forward your newsletter to friends and others who may be interested in the material. This form of marketing, known as *viral marketing*, is often the most successful as we trust those who have made the recommendation so read the e-mail as opposed to deleting an unsolicited one. You encourage flow by offering incentives. For example: 'If you bring a friend or partner, two places are available at the conference for this reduced price.'

- **Reach out** – to groups or individuals, industry bodies, etc. that you think might want to make your newsletter available to others.

- **Consider buying a list**. There are many companies that sell vast quantities of contact details or handle mailings for one-off use. The benefit of this is that you have access to a far wider network of people than you could acquire yourself. The negative side is that you will have no prior relationships with those individuals so it will be significantly harder to build them up; the cost of purchase is a significant factor; and such individuals may have information overload from being on commercial lists.

Some companies also offer discount vouchers for referrals that then become customers. If using referrals, it is important that you track where the person heard about you and that you thank the referrer. This can be done on your website form or at check-out by asking, 'Where did you hear about us?' It also allows you to monitor the effectiveness of your networking strategy.

CHAPTER 20

Manage your
network

Establish regular contact times

If you have critical business contacts it might be worth scheduling one lunch a month and a bi-weekly phone call. If they are former work colleagues, appropriate contact might be to organise drinks every three or six months. It is important that you prioritise. A good contact management system like Outlook lets you set up reminders that help you keep up a consistent contact process.

Manage expectations

If you know that you cannot respond to all e-mails from those who respond to your newsletter be sure to clarify how communication will be handled. Do not put your personal e-mail or phone number on your website unless you are prepared to take calls at all times. If you feel that you cannot commit to regular attendance at a particular network's meetings then be honest with yourself and upfront with the network organisers.

Be consistent

If you promise a monthly newsletter make sure that it does not get sent every two months, or even worse *haphazardly*. A common mistake with networking is biting off more than you can chew. As you grow your network and database you must devise

devise a clear communication strategy for keeping in contact

a clear communication strategy for keeping in contact. Without this, the danger is that you get overworked, soon the network becomes a burden and finally it gets sacrificed. Without sufficient due care the network can break down and you can lose trust.

Delegate

If you have a team, share responsibility for maintaining network contact. This could mean dividing regular contacts between team members, allowing individuals to take turns in editing the newsletter and presenting new features. Members of the team can also be representatives of your company in different network forums. This can add vibrancy to your network communications and contacts and gives you fresh perspectives.

Use tracking tools for your website and newsletter

Most website hosts now provide a range of data regarding when you receive the most hits on your website, where the people live, down to their income bracket. Use these data to shape your contact with your network by seeing how many people visit you, how many forward on your e-newsletter, and how many click on links within it.

Look after yourself

Sometimes we can be so busy looking after the needs of others that we forget about planning time for ourselves and looking after our own well-being. Make sure that your goals for growing your network do not clash with other goals and priorities such as spending time with those you care for, as well as looking after yourself.

brilliant example

The famous psychotherapist Carl Jung was always surrounded at every conference by people asking for some of his time. A particularly important woman wanted to meet him on a specified day but Jung replied he had a meeting at that time. The day came and the woman was walking in the park when she saw Jung reading by the river with his feet in the water. This was at the same time he had told her he had a meeting. She was furious, ran up to Jung and shouted, 'You lied to me, you said you had a meeting'. Jung replied calmly, 'I do, it is with myself!'

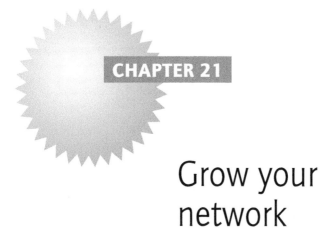

CHAPTER 21

Grow your
network

The skill of brilliant networkers is that their network does not remain static, but grows and develops, adding value and creating more opportunities. There are some very straight-forward ways to extend your network and build your database.

Extending your network

Volunteer to speak at conferences and events

There are dozens of conferences happening every day, with many conference organisers struggling to find speakers. By keeping a look out for conferences in your field you can be proactive by contacting organisers in advance to let them know you are available to speak on a topic. If you have an e-brochure or newsletter it might also be worth sending them a copy.

brilliant tip

Speaking at conferences establishes credibility but it also gives you the opportunity to connect with other experts in your field and the audience who might be potential clients or partners. Take the opportunity at a conference not only to network with your fellow speakers but to speak to people from the audience, and take questions in the break or after the event.

Work on an organising committee

In most networking organisations and professional bodies there is an organising committee. Volunteer to contribute to that committee. Again, it will increase your exposure and standing, giving you access to new people or opportunities.

Become an author

Write articles for the newsletters of any groups you belong to or industry magazines. These could be as simple as ten top tips in your specialist subject. Often these can be taken from your own e-newsletter, avoiding you duplicating work. At the end of the article ensure you list your website address or mention a free newsletter with the link.

Start your own network

Often we might not find a group of people that meets our exact needs. In this case it might be useful to think about setting one up.

brilliant example

Carole Stone, who now has 30,000 people on her database, runs and coordinates regular events. She says:

It can be helpful to hold what I call a 'salon', an informal gathering of friends and colleagues, say once a week, for just an hour and a half; no shorter, or people will miss meeting each other. It could be from 6pm to 7.30pm in a room above a pub with a cash bar; or from 12.30pm to 2pm in a room in your office where you could provide a few bottles of inexpensive wine and some water. Try it for say four or six weeks. E-mail colleagues and friends you'd like to be there and invite anyone you meet that week who you'd like to see again – encourage people to bring someone along with them.
The important thing is that the 'salon' is on the same day at the same time in the same place. This keeps you in touch and helps you meet new people.

Speed networking

Another way you can grow your network is by hosting speed networking events. Speed networking is a bit like speed dating. You talk to the person next to you for three minutes about your business or idea, then move on to someone else when the whistle blows.

> speed networking is a bit like speed dating

Below are some tips provided by Oli Barrett, an expert, on why and how he hosts successful speed networking events.

brilliant tip

Why speed network?

It's a great way to bring people together from a wide range of industries – that's what you need when you're starting up a venture. I've brought thousands of people together since then and I still love hosting them.

Why did you start running networking events?

A great guy called Mike Grenville let me experiment with it during one of his own events – he'd had a speaker pull out at the last minute.

That gave me the confidence to hold an event of my own, and I invited everyone in my network. Because it was an early weekday night, I found certain venues would give me a room for free, so the events didn't cost anything. I collected the positive comments from the first event and added them to the bottom of the second invitation.

Overall the benefits of starting your own event far outweigh the costs. Most opportunities come from people we know slightly. So it's a fun and smart way of keeping in touch and leads to you attracting loads of opportunities. Finally, you create goodwill across hundreds of people which can be helpful further in the future. Try it!

Have you any tips for hosting an event?

1   Spend some time before the event sitting down with a quick cup of tea and a printed guest list and thinking about any of the potential introductions you could make in the room.

2   Once you've introduced two people, give a brief line to each about the other ('John's a keen fisherman', and 'I met Sandy on a beach'), then don't be afraid to just walk away without any big 'goodbye'.

3   Make early friends with the venue team as they'll be a great source of support as the evening goes by. It's never good to have to introduce yourself at the point something has gone wrong. More than a quick 'hi', it's really worth having a proper chat early on.

4   At the end of the event, remind the guests that you're happy to introduce them to any of the guests they didn't have time to chat to. The best thing of all is that once people think of you as someone who knows people, then that in turn attracts opportunities.

Networking groups for small businesses

Opposite is a story of a young entrepreneur, Patrick Philpott, ambassador for EDGE, who started up a local business network and now runs Vision Path events (**www.visionpath. co.uk**). Here he shares how he set up his network.

▶ brilliant example

I set up Intelligent Networking on the Hertfordshire/Essex borders in September 2005 to provide a forum for local businesses to network effectively without having to fork out several hundreds of pounds per year for membership to larger organisations.

What was particularly telling, and helped me identify the need for a new business network in my area, was that despite it being an immensely commerce-rich area there was nothing available apart from ad hoc events staged by local accountancy firms and the local chapter of a much larger networking organisation. Good networking events were conspicuous by their absence, and I felt it was time for that to change.

The way in which I set about creating Intelligent Networking and staging its first event was through tapping into my extensive network of contacts, finding out their opinions of what makes a good networking event, and then taking the key elements and incorporating them into my own functions. This meant I had a strong structure to my events, always had two short speeches based on a theme relevant to the local business community, and then laid on the ubiquitous drinks that allowed for informal networking to take place after the formality of the speeches.

When promoting your network, try to cultivate a contact at your local newspaper and with a local councillor or MP. Often, they will have personal networks of local professionals and business people and will be happy to write to them asking them for their support by attending your new networking event(s).

A warning however: networking events are time consuming, costly and often heavily reliant on external influences. Even the weather can deter people from attending a networking event! So be prepared for a lot of hard work, dedication and you'll need endless tenacity. But if you can devote the time to the cause, you'll make a success of establishing a new network in your area.

CHAPTER 22

Networking in organisations

etworks are not just about building external relationships, they can also involve building internal relationships within your existing company and workplace. This can be with people below you, at your level and with your boss and others above you.

Below are some pointers to help you network successfully at work.

Networking with those below you

Often the gate keepers of any organisation are the staff on the ground who can grant you access and move the earth to support you if you have a good relationship, and are able to block you if you do not. So consider the following:

- A key tip to networking with those below you is always remember that the person deserves your full respect and courtesy, irrespective of what role they perform. You can display this by saying thank you, greeting by first name and making a point to start an informal friendly conversation.

- Another way to support those below you is to mentor them. Often there is a chain in organisations that is highly unpredictable. The person might be below you now but in a few years they might be your manager for various reasons. Mentoring by informally offering support, guidance or information regularly not only keeps you plugged in to what is happening beneath you in the organisation but also helps develop talent upwards.

brilliant tip

Be careful how you treat people on your way up – you can expect to receive similar treatment from them in return on your way down! (An old adage.)

● Try to create a positive atmosphere when relating to others below you so that they feel comfortable in approaching you. Not only when things go right but also admitting to mistakes when things go wrong. By having this confidence in you, you will gain an added advantage over your peers who might not have the same information or trust with those below.

Networking with those at your level

This requires different skills, as follows:

● In most organisations there are social activities. Sometimes these are very informal and might revolve around going to the bar after work. This might not be everyone's idea of fun but if you have no objections to alcohol it might be worth going along as often friendships are made in this way.

● If you do object to alcohol for personal or religious reasons it is very important you find other ways that you can build relationships with your colleagues. This might be at a sports club, it might be through being on the employee forum or through other groups.

networking is not nepotism

brilliant **tip**

If you feel that networking only revolves around the bar or evening events and that this is having an adverse impact on your career in terms of networking, make sure you raise your concerns with your mentor or a manager.

Suggest alternatives for team activities. After all there are other people, such as those who have parenting and caring responsibilities, who might also be excluded from after-work networking activities.

If you notice that you are not being treated in a fair manner solely because you are not networking, for example, being given lower status projects than peers who do network, then again it is important you raise your concerns with your manager. Networking is not nepotism. While access to people does improve your ability to be noticed and compete, equally it is the organisation's responsibility to be meritocratic and transparent.

- Volunteer yourself on to cross-business committees or task forces. Often these give you the opportunity to meet people from other departments with a clear business focus. This also serves as a tool for mobility as if you are thinking of moving within your company you at least have got a contact who can provide you with information.

- Form or join an employee network. Many large companies, especially multinationals, run employee networks that are funded by the company. These tend to be for diverse groups that are under-represented within the firm but often they are open to anybody to attend. For example, Jane Terry is a co-chair of the Women's Leadership Network for a large bank. Started two years ago it now has over 800 members. The mission of the network is to promote the recruitment, development and retention of women within the firm. She shares her six top tips for an effective employee network:

brilliant tips

Jane Terry's top six

1 **Have co-chairs.** Leading a network is a voluntary job, above and beyond your day job. It takes considerable time and leadership. Having a co-chair ensures that the responsibility is not just on one person's shoulders and it gives you the flexibility to share tough times when business demands mean you cannot be so present for the network.

2 **Have a cross-business committee.** It helps when starting a network to ensure that all parts of your business are represented. This way the whole firm is connected and you are able to agree initiatives that will support everybody.

3 **Ensure senior sponsorship.** For networks to succeed they need the direct backing of senior management. Our committee meets for an hour every fortnight but between that we are very busy organising events and planning initiatives. It's important you have support, ideally from the board, and they are in favour of your aims.

4 **Profile your network.** When you have a network, marketing your activities is essential. It's important that your network is seen as mainstream and that people know who to connect to for more information, especially at the committee level. Using the company intranet is a useful tool to do this.

5 **Ensure inclusivity.** Networks should be open to all. Although we have a women's network we have a male senior sponsor and events are open to everyone across the firm. It's important that all networks are used to bring people together, not to divide.

6 **Check regularly what your members want.** Networks exist for the benefit of the members, not the committee, and it pays to constantly seek feedback after you do events and when planning strategy. You can also involve members in sub-groups working on tasks, which keeps you focused on members' needs.

- Networking Fridays. Not all of us work in large companies; we might be in a medium-sized company which is just too big to get to know everyone but not big enough to have funding for employee networks. A simple idea to starting up a network is to create a time in the week when people can meet at a certain location. This might be at morning coffee time, say 10.30 every Friday at the canteen. If there is no space internally it might be at a local venue on a certain lunchtime every week. With no formal agenda this just presents the opportunity for people to connect informally.

- Join cross-industry networks. Most industries have cross-industry forums or networks. Again, research these on the Web. They are brilliant ways to get to meet people at your level across different companies. If there is no forum for your role it might be worth exploring and contacting your peers to see if they are interested in setting one up. Most companies are keen to participate as they recognise the value of benchmarking with competitors, sharing information on best practice, raising the profile of their industry and also negotiating jointly with suppliers.

Networking with those above you

We might think that it is important to network at our level but if we only do this, with no connection to those above us, it is far harder to succeed than if we consciously network upwards. Here are a few pointers for doing that:

- There is a maxim that says 'Don't dress for the role you are in but dress for the role you aspire to'. This can be changed to 'Make sure you build a network for the career level or position you aspire to'.

- While organisations are getting flatter, at least on paper, hierarchies still exist. The first step in networking upwards **is being aware of those above you and how they are**

connected. It makes sense to find out who your bosses report to, who they meet and who they connect with. You might find it useful to draw a network map, as suggested earlier, to illustrate this connection.

brilliant tip

Once you have identified who the key managers are for your career path, do a bit of research into their teams. Often this can be done on the company intranet. **What are the pressing issues on their minds?** Are there any changes in legislation that will affect them? If you don't have access to them directly, it might be worth speaking to members of their teams who might be at your level.

● Having found some information, the simple key is to **connect with useful information**. This might be to send superiors details of a course with a note saying 'Thought you might be interested. This might be useful for the team dealing with changes in legislation'.

● It is important at this level to keep the message short, clear and helpful. Do not over-communicate. As a guideline wait for feedback, but if you receive none, do not worry. If the information was truly helpful it will have been noted.

● Never go above your immediate boss with a request to their manager or another senior manager without letting your boss know; or provide any information that is likely to upset or is confidential to your team. The likely result is that this will become known and cause resentment.

networking is not a forum to express grievances

If you have a problem, going above your boss might bring you results but it will most likely damage your career development in the longer term. Networking is not a forum to express grievances.

- Becoming an expert is another way to network with those above you. If you have learnt how to manage the internal website it is likely that you will be a go-to person when information needs to be posted.

- Find a mentor. Perhaps the most useful way to network with those above you is to find a mentor for guidance. This can be done formally or informally, and your mentor does not necessarily need to be in your department. Often a mentor will let you know of opportunities to be on committees or sub-groups that will give you exposure to those above you and they will also act as an advocate to support you.

- Approach people. While maintaining professionalism, it is important to approach people. Often senior managers do want to connect with those at all levels of their organisation as they know this is how they keep in touch with what is happening in the business. Have the confidence to approach them and to start a conversation based on thoughtful questions.

- Think wide as well as deep. During periods of organisational change network structures can alter very quickly. By having a wide pool of contacts with strong relationships across the business and at all levels you have a wider support network to draw upon to manage transitions.

If you find that you have a new manager, immediately apply the principles of this book. The only thing certain about the past is it is the past, so you need to be able to move on and create your network anew. Hopefully the tools in this book will help you do so much more quickly.

brilliant tip

Make a list of four or five people in your company who you consider role models or who you would like to learn from. Send them an open e-mail asking if they could spare the time to meet you for coffee as you are seeking informal advice. Often you might be surprised that people are genuinely interested in helping. If they agree to the meeting make sure you are well prepared and ask thoughtful questions so they can share their experience. Also send a follow-up e-mail to thank them for their time.

CHAPTER 23

Bonus chapter:
Social capital –
success is social

Often books on networking focus simply on 'personal networking'. In this chapter you will discover what social capital is and how the structure, size and diversity of your network can impact on your success. We will also explore practical tools that you may use to assess your social capital or use within your own team or organisation.

What does it take to be successful?

In his brilliant book *Achieving Success through Social Capital* the author Wayne Baker, Professor of Organisational Behaviour at the University of Michigan, recounts that he frequently asks people the question 'What does it take to be successful in your personal and professional lives?'

I have since posed the question to many groups when speaking about networking. The most frequent answers I got back were talent, intelligence, hard work, education and even luck! Yet as Baker, who got similar answers, points out, behind all these answers is one basic assumption: that success is the result of individual skills, effort and capabilities. He calls this the 'myth of individualism'.

A closer examination paints a broader picture than our myth of the 'heroic individual' that has pervaded our interest in western society and has led to many a book on the heroic leader. This has recently been called into question by the growing sense that even our heroic leaders are as fragile and as fallible as we are. Equally, each of them relies on others, sometimes many others, to help them achieve their success.

Take the quality 'natural talent'. Although the current US President Obama is a gifted orator his memorable speeches and catch phrases 'Yes we can' are not simply a result of his natural penmanship or creative mind. He has a young speech writer, Jon Favreau, who devises his speeches, and directs a whole team that works together to craft every word and advise Obama on delivery.

Or take intelligence. Perhaps people will bring Einstein to mind as an iconic manifestation of the word. Yet we know that as a child Einstein was considered to have learning difficulties. Studies have been done to illustrate a Pygmalion effect: that teachers' perceptions affect students' performance, but also how the peer group can have an impact on performance. The idea that IQ (intelligence quotient) alone can measure intelligence has been challenged, and some educational experts, like Howard Gardner, propose multiple intelligences, including interpersonal intelligence or social intelligence. Daniel Goleman, who developed the concept of emotional intelligence, has recently written about ecological intelligence – a sign of our times!

Education is always a quality that people associate with success. If someone has a first degree, PhD, an MBA or the right qualification in their industry, then this will assist them in being successful! While there is a correlation with educational attainment and income, access to education in itself is also socially determined. For example, depending on whether you are male or female in some parts of the world can determine your access to education as much as whether you are the first child or the second born and money needs to be brought in to feed the family. Access to books, resources, low classroom sizes, brilliant teachers, and after school support are all influenced by geography, socio-economic status, and a variety of factors beyond individual ability or the desire to learn. Education rarely happens in a social vacuum and many complex factors are involved.

> education rarely happens in a social vacuum

Surely success comes through personal determination and effort? Edison is often quoted as saying 'Success is 1% inspiration and 99% perspiration'. When I think of determination and sheer effort an image of polar explorers comes to mind. Yet even they, while they may walk unassisted to as far flung climes as the North Pole, would in fact credit whole teams who prepared them, monitored them and were ready to rescue them if the odd polar bear or two attacked!

Luck is probably the last answer I receive. Yet even luck is not as random as we think. The psychologist Professor Richard Wiseman, author of *Are You Lucky?*, at the University of Hertfordshire did a ten-year study into the science of luck. He concluded that to a large extent luck is created and that it is possible to enhance the amount of luck people have in their lives. Factors such as 'positive expectations' can impact on luck and act as self-fulfilling prophecies. Access to new ideas can also influence opportunity and we shall see later how diversity in the composition of your network is key for creativity.

Current research also shows how even emotions like happiness can be influenced by people in your network and dispositions are not as random as we think. Nicholas Christakis and James Fowler in their book *Connected: Amazing Power of Social Networks and How They Shape Our Lives* (2010) argue that although most of us realise how our actions can affect those closest to us, for example the feelings, health and wealth of families and friends, their research shows that the influence we have by everything we think, feel, do and say, can affect people far beyond our direct contact. Discovering a '3 degrees rule', the idea that influence spreads through at least 3 degrees of separation, then just having 20 contacts who are randomly connected to 20 others in the same way, and their contacts who are equally connected (20 × 20 × 20), can mean influencing 8000 people! Their research shows how networks influence the spread of joy, the search for partners, keeping health and promoting democracy, but at the same time can also spread depression, obesity, financial panic and violence. In answer to the questions 'Can your friends make you fat?' or 'Can your siblings make you smart?' they show compelling evidence of how the structure of networks can be an influence. Christakis and Fowler say, 'As part of a social network, we transcend ourselves, for good or ill, and become part of something much larger. We are connected' (2010, p. 30).

The argument of this chapter is that success is also social. It depends on our networks as much as it does on our individual efforts and abilities. We shall look at studies that show that

> the argument of this chapter is that success is also social

your pay, promotion and even your performance review can be influenced by the structure and composition of your network. This is radical thinking and perhaps best expressed in Mohammed Ali's short poem: we need to keep in mind that success is a both/and a: 'Me We'.

brilliant definition

Social capital is the concept that value can be created from the structure, quality, size and diversity of your networks, whether personal or professional.

So what is social capital?

This value may be in the form of connections, job opportunities or intangibles such as support or creativity. What distinguishes social capital from human capital (value created by individual skills and knowledge), Baker argues, is that the value in social capital does not reside in any one individual but rather in the network of the relationships. Like any other capital it creates value.

We shall explore some more nuances of social capital further in this chapter but let's take a look at why social capital may be relevant to you.

Why is social capital relevant to you?

There are several reasons why you may want to focus on social capital. See how many apply to you:

- You want to increase collaboration in your team and you suspect that cooperation is not happening as widely as you want it to.

- You need to manage across different boundaries, time zones and geographies with people in more than one location.

- Although you have to lead you possess very little formal 'authority' and need to get things done through informal authority, through relationships with others.

- There is diversity in your team and you want to drive value from these differences.

- Your organisation, department or team has recently merged with another and you want to find out how to navigate in the new structure.

- You appreciate that your promotion relies on your influence not only with your manager but with your colleagues and your relationships with them.

● You want to become more valuable as a connector and learn skills that can help you get promoted faster, earn more money and receive better appraisals.

Whether you work in a start up, SME or global company, it is likely that you will all face challenges regarding diversity, growth and needing to influence. The advantage of social capital is that it allows us to manage our networks consciously. Baker argues that it is our ethical responsibility to tend to our relationships as much as we do to other areas of life.

So having recognised the importance of social capital and how it may be of benefit, how do you measure your social capital? To do that we need to use a bit of magic – or at least a tool, called a social network analysis (SNA), developed by some clever sociologists!

Making the invisible visible

Think of any company you know. Most of them, if not all, will have an organisational chart. It might look something like this:

Yet we all know that information in organisations rarely follows the linear nature of charts. For example if Bill wants something done he might know not to go to his manager but instead to a colleague who has more influence. We know that there are certain people in organisations who are leaders and key to making things happen, even if they do not hold any formal visible leadership position (positional authority). In the same way there are people who can block information by withholding or acting as a bottleneck: 'all the approvals need to go through me' syndrome.

The reality of most organisations is that information and relationships are far more complex and dynamic than the formal organisation chart. Instead they may look something like this:

Source: Figure 1.1 from Burt, R. (2005) *Brokerage and Closure: An Introduction to Social Capital*, Oxford University Press, Oxford, p. 14. Reprinted with permission.

If the figure above looks complicated it will be made simple in a few moments. It is an example of an SNA diagram, a pictorial representation of the relationships between people, rather than formal organisational structures.

This SNA of an organisation comes from a book, *Brokerage and Closure*, by Professor Ron Burt, at the University of Chicago Booth. Burt, a world leading academic in the field of social capital, makes the point that all organisations have a social history. When people come into an organisation they are coming into a complex set of relationships typically finding their place within a small group or cluster. We can think of clusters as formed by people who are in frequent contact; perhaps teams, departments or comprising of people who connect frequently due to a particular affinity (e.g. job role, function and social reasons). Sociograms are created through a process of interviews or questionnaires where people identify who they are most connected to and relate to, where they go to get things done, etc.

In the diagram above each dot represents a person. The dotted lines represent 'weak ties' – a relationship between two people that is not strong. The thicker the line, the stronger the relationship, so a solid line is a 'strong tie'. (We discussed this briefly in Chapter 10.) You can see that there are more connections inside of clusters than between them, which seems to indicate 'white space' or a lack of connection. These represent gaps in the information flow.

As part of the diagram you will see that in the box a small cluster has been made more visible for illustration purposes. Here you can see the connections between two people, James and Robert. Although they both seem to have the same number of connections, each six strong ties and one weak tie, they are both connected in remarkably different ways.

density denotes how many of the people within the network know each other

From the diagram you can see that James is connected to everyone within cluster B, whether directly or going through one of his direct contacts. As everyone is connected to each other this would be known as a 'closed' network, with reasonably high density. Density denotes how many of the people within the network know each other.

Robert's network has a very different structure to James'. Although he is connected to cluster B, through his contact with contact 7, he is the closest contact between cluster B and cluster A, and through his relationship with contact 6 he is also the only contact between cluster B and clusters C and D. In this network Robert has a 'bridge' relationship which Burt argues is an example of 'brokerage'.

It is this ability of brokerage that Burt argues gives Robert more social capital than James. Social capital is created by the ability to bridge structural holes or disconnects, to create value. Although it may seem both Robert and James have the same number of contacts, Robert has three main advantages over James:

- diversity
- speed
- information arbitrage.

Diversity

Firstly Robert has access to a greater diversity of information. He not only knows what is happening in cluster B but also has information about what is happening in clusters A, C and D. This information allows him to be more informed of changes or information that may affect him. It allows him to have access to a greater number of domains of knowledge, therefore allowing the possibility of creativity by combining ideas to create new solutions.

Contrast this with James' network where he has high density. The benefits of people knowing each other may lead to a lot of trust. The reason being is that if one person were to act in a way that damaged group relations it would be likely that everyone else would know, quickly, and there would be some form of regulation by the group. This could also be a disadvantage in that because they are so closely connected conflict would be harder and therefore the value of differences would be more difficult to benefit from. In teams this could result in 'group think' where ideas are adopted early and agreed by the whole group, without much challenge, even though they may not be the best ideas.

Another problem of high density is that although it may lead to good close team work, important for routine tasks, it lacks 'news of difference' and therefore can lead to information redundancy, self-absorption, and the inability to respond to circumstances of change outside of the group. Robert by being both connected within the group and also to external sources of input is less likely to develop this group think. Over time it is also likely that people in Robert's networks will get to know each other, hence their density will increase.

Does size matter?

'The bigger the better' is often an implicit assumption when it comes to size! We all know people who might have a few hundred friends on Facebook or in their personal or professional network, but does size really matter?

Take a look at the following diagram:

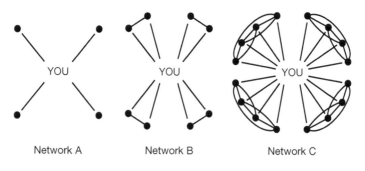

Network A   Network B   Network C

Source: Adapted from Figure 1.2, Burt, R. (2005) *Brokerage and Closure: An Introduction to Social Capital*, Oxford University Press, Oxford, p. 21. Reprinted with permission.

It is a diagram that illustrates the number of contacts you develop after starting a new job. The question is: which network diagram has access to the most information? In Network A you have four contacts, in Network B they double to eight and in Network C double again to 16. The most frequent answer is that you have more access to more information in Network C as there are more people, hence more ideas. The assumption is again being made that information resides in individuals rather than in access to the fields of knowledge or networks that each person has access to. In this diagram, the information level has actually stayed the same! There remain four fields of information but the difference is that you will need to keep in touch with 16 people in Network C to reach the same knowledge as in Network A.

brilliant example

What is the connection between a termite hill and an office building? Well the British architect Mick Pearce was given a challenge by Old Mutual, an insurance and real estate company, to build a functioning office building in the middle of Harare, Zimbabwe. The challenge was to use no air conditioning even though temperatures could get as high as 100 degrees by day and as low as 40 degrees by night! Pearce, who was born in Zimbabwe, did this by basing his design on how termites cool their dirt and mud towers by directing cool wind from the base into opening and closing chambers and ducts to reach the peak. By doing this they are able to keep a steady temperature of 73 to 77 degrees. The result of combining his insight into termite ecosystems and his architectural training was the Eastgate building – the largest commercial and retail complex in Harare that instantly saved Old Mutual $3.5 million as the company did not have to install air conditioning and uses 10 per cent of the energy of other buildings its size.

The key therefore is not simply to look only for size but also to look for diversity and difference. Diversity is the key for developing social capital. In

diversity is the key
for developing
social capital

his book *The Medici Effect*, Frans Johanssen gives many examples of how individuals and teams that seek diversity and step into the intersection between fields, disciplines or cultures, combining ideas, are more creative and innovative in finding solutions.

An example of a high-performing team that builds diversity into its structural composition is the world's leading design firm IDEO, which is responsible for a host of innovations from the first mouse for Apple to the world's first laptop computer to the mechanical whale in the film *Free Willy*. By recruiting for diverse domain knowledge (e.g. doctors and psychologists work alongside architects and artists) they are able to benefit from creating brokerage and bridging information holes all within one team. Watch the IDEO team on Nightline being challenged to completely redesign a shopping cart. Note how they have a process of innovation that benefits from diversity (**http:// www.youtube.com/watch?v=M66ZU2PCIcM**).

brilliant tip

The rule is simple: when building your network you need to think diversity as well as size. Ask, 'What additional diversity will this new contact bring to my network?' There is a story told of Henry Ford who is reported to have said, 'Show me two men with the same skills and ability and I'll show you one man I don't need!'

Speed

A second advantage that Robert has over James is that due to where he is positioned in his network he has early access to information and is probably the first to hear about changes. This gives him the ability to adapt earlier than others to take advantage of the information. This 'first mover' advantage can be critical in making necessary changes in good time. In some industries, for example, financial services and trading, even microseconds in information delay can mean the difference in who is the first to trade, and can correspond to fortunes being made, or lost!

Information arbitrage

The third advantage Robert has over James is what Burt calls 'information arbitrage'. Robert will know when it is of value to connect people in his diverse networks to create value, but importantly because only he has this knowledge it gives him a disproportionate say in whose interests are being served. It can be argued that Robert's advantage does not rely just on his connections but on his ability to detect and maintain bridge relationships. He possesses the skills to go between the different worlds and to help them communicate with each other.

An example might be network A as finance and network B as sales and marketing. Each would have its own language, whether 'profit and loss' or 'customer proposition', or more frequently TLAs – three letter acronyms, which for speed and familiarity lead to a feeling of 'we know what we are talking about' but also exclusion to those who don't speak that language. Robert is in a unique position as he has the skills of 'translation' to act not only as a bridge in language but also in cultures, making him a valuable connector.

Why does it matter to be a 'bridge' or broker?

This may all seem interesting information, but does it really matter to you? Well, research by Burt shows that it does: all things being equal, people with 'bridge' structures in their network earn more, are promoted faster and receive more favourable job evaluations than those with closed networks.

Below is a table from Burt, used by Professor Raider in her teaching on 'The Competitive Advantage of Social Capital', showing the correlation between networks across different industries and the above measures of success.

Executives	Industry	Outcome	Findings
A & B. Supply Chain Leaders & Managers	Defence & Aerospace	Salary, Job Evaluations, Promotion & Raise	• Bridges increase salary • Bridges increase likelihood of favourable job evaluation • Dense, interconnected networks increase the likelihood of poor job evaluation
C. Functional Managers	Financial Service Firms	Job Evaluations	• Bridges increase likelihood of favourable job evaluation • Dense, interconnected networks increase likelihood of poor job evaluation
D. Senior Executives	Computer/ Electronics	Fast Track Promotion	• Bridges increase speed of promotion
E. Investment Bankers	Financial Services	Year-End Bonus	• Bridges increase annual bonus
F. French Managers	Chemical & Pharm.	Salary	• Bridges increase salary

G. Asia Pacific Senior Executives/ All Functions	Computer Hardware	Salary	• Bridges increase salary
H. Engineering Teams	Manufacturing	TQM Team Awards	• Bridges increase quality in TQM initiatives

Source: Burt, R. (2005) *Brokerage and Closure: An Introduction to Social Capital*, Oxford University Press, Oxford, p. 37. Table used by Professor H. Raider, based on this source.

The key here is not to make either type of network 'right' or 'wrong' but to see that each has different advantages and disadvantages. Either may be most useful in different circumstances and leaders need to be adept at developing skills to create and maintain both types of network relationships. This has led to the concept of 'T'-shaped leadership.

T-shaped leadership

In their 2001 *Harvard Business Review* article 'Introducing T-Shaped Managers', Hansen and von Oetinger introduce the concept of managers cultivating 'T'-shaped networks, indicating that, like the vertical bar in the T shape, they have depth in their networks and a focus on their unit's performance but also like the horizontal bar across the top, they have breadth and reach out across their own cluster to others to share their ideas and expertise across the company.

Hansen and von Oetinger's research shows that cross-unit collaboration increases efficiency, improves decision quality, grows revenue through shared expertise and helps develop new ideas through cross-pollination of ideas. They argue that companies should encourage 'portals', which are individuals who connect those who need information with those who have it – their term for brokers or connectors!

How do I measure my own social capital and that of my team or organisation?

By now you might be eager to understand more about your social capital, to discover:

- Who's in your core network?
- How are they connected?
- What is the strength of your social capital?
- Where do you need to build and invest?

Fortunately there are online tools to help you do this and all you need is an internet connection. One particular tool I recommend is the *Humax Assessment* for an accurate – and revealing – picture of your social network, profile type and diagnostics. One advantage is that once you've completed the assessment, you instantly get your customised results online!

To complete the survey visit **www.humaxnetworks.com**. You will find plenty more tools there for developing and measuring social capital. Readers of *Brilliant networking* get a discount by entering the special code found on page 270 of this book.

Breaking down silos

Hopefully, after completing the Humax survey, you will have a deeper understanding of your own social capital at an individual level. Let's take a look at what benefits doing an SNA in an organisation can bring.

SNA can be a very effective tool for promoting collaboration and knowledge sharing within important groups such as the core functions of an organisation, research and development departments, or strategic business units.

Rob Cross and Andrew Parker, authors of *The Hidden Power of Social Networks: Understanding How Work* Really *Gets Done in Organisations* (2004), give an example of a highly skilled group that was commissioned to provide thought leadership and specialised support to their organisation's knowledge management consultants.

The members of the group had either advanced degrees or extensive industry experience in strategy and organisational design or in technical fields such as data warehousing or information architecture. The partner who was leading this group thought that by bringing the two specialised skill sets together the firm could provide a more integrated holistic solution and distinguish itself from competitors. Yet he felt that the group was not working together as well as he would have liked so he conducted a SNA. The results of information sharing before implementing any changes are shown below:

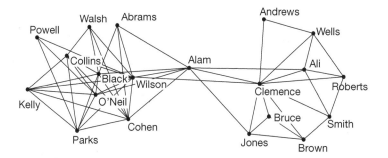

Source: Figure 3-1a from R. Cross *et al.* (2002) 'Making invisible work visible: using social network analysis to support strategic collaboration', *California Management Review* 44(2): 25–46. Copyright ©2002, by The Regents of the University of California. By permission of The Regents.

Cross's analysis confirmed the partner's intuition. As shown in the figure above, the information sharing network revealed not one group at all but two distinct sub-groups.

The group on the left-hand side of the network was skilled in the 'softer' issues of strategy or organisational design, often focusing on cultural interventions or other aspects of organisations to help improve knowledge creation and sharing. The group on the right-hand side was composed of people skilled in 'harder' technical aspects of knowledge management such as information architecture, modelling and data warehousing.

Over time, members of these two sub-groups had gravitated towards each other. This was because of common projects, attending the same conferences, reading the same journals, etc. The problem was that neither group knew the skill set of the

> the problem was that neither group knew the skill set of the other

other and therefore did not know who to involve in joint pitches or project teams. You will notice one individual (Alam) in the middle, who did connect the two groups. Alam was a skilled technical specialist in technology but due to an MBA and other experiences he was able to bridge the two worlds. He was also the highest performer and on track to become a partner. Although Alam had the potential to be a bridge, in this case he acted as a block to collaboration, telling each side that he was essential to work through and not to bother with collaborating with the others.

After the SNA, the team sat down and discussed what they could now see visibly. Alam was acting as a bottleneck rather than being a broker. After a lengthy facilitated discussion they put in three simple measures such as ensuring internal projects were jointly staffed, using mixed revenue sales goals which had both a technical and organisational component, and increasing communication channels (e.g. through a weekly e-bulletin and project tracking database). The result was that people had access to the information and the knowledge of everybody in the network, allowing them to work together.

The team over the next several months began to work in a more integrated fashion and sold more business. An SNA conducted by Cross nine months later showed a very different pattern of connections!

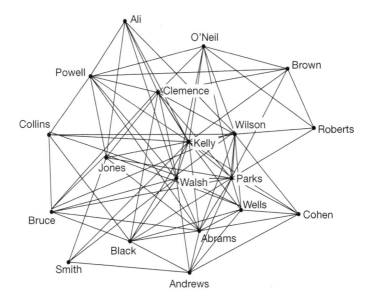

Source: Figure 3-1b from R. Cross *et al.* (2002) 'Making invisible work visible: using social network analysis to support strategic collaboration', *California Management Review* 44(2): 25–46. Copyright ©2002, by The Regents of the University of California. By permission of The Regents.

The above is an example of how SNA can encourage collaboration across boundaries even when barriers may not be obviously visible. Networks can be used to divide as well as to connect and leaders have an ethical responsibility to manage their relationships and networks responsibly.

What are some of the practical things that I can do to become a T-shaped leader?

brilliant tips

1 Conduct your own SNA using the tool from Humax. If you are also able to do this with your team or organisation, do so and discuss the results with each other or use a facilitator to explore the issues in more detail.

2 From your network analysis take the time to develop closer relationships within your team but also make a conscious effort to get to know people outside of your existing team or domain of knowledge. Practise making the most of existing networking opportunities, as in Chapter 22, and if you can't join a network – start one!

3 Realise that networks are not static, and an SNA is only one snapshot in a point of time. Networks need constant attention and it pays to continually revisit your network analysis. Pay attention not only to who is on your SNA, but also importantly who is not. Often customers and suppliers are conspicuously missing!

CHAPTER 24

Bonus chapter: Over to you! Networking activities

As a result of the first edition of *Brilliant networking* I received many e-mails from readers asking for practical activities that they could do to help people to get to know each other at networking events and to practise networking skills.

Here are a couple of favourites that I and close friends in my network use. You can use and adapt them to suit the needs of your own group – experiment and enjoy!

All change!

- **Purpose**: To enable people to break out of cliques and to get to know each other very quickly. To raise energy in the room.
- **Number of people**: 15+.
- **Equipment**: Stopwatch and whistle. A clear space where people can move easily. A glass of something to drink!

How to run it

This is one of my favourite activities as it can be done almost anywhere and once it starts it really raises the noise levels and buzz in the room. It is derived from Oli Barrett, a master in speed networking activities (**www.dailynetworker.co.uk**).

This activity is best done at the end of a meeting or function when you then want people to mingle and stay longer connecting. Start by inviting people to grab a drink – a glass in one hand always helps conversation to flow – but hot drinks are not recommended as there will be a lot of moving around!

Then introduce the activity as an opportunity to get to meet more people, so that maybe a valuable connection can be made. There are three rules to making the activity work. Describe them to the group.

- Rule 1: They have to meet someone new that they did not come with or have not met before.

- Rule 2: They will only have two minutes together and they can talk about anything they want. It's not about hard core deal making or doing business.

- Rule 3: At the end of the two minutes a whistle will be blown and they must change partners – no double dating!

brilliant tip

Mention to the group that once the activity starts they may find that everyone else is paired up except them. When that happens it is important not to slope off and use it as an excuse to quickly disappear to the bathroom, or stand alone feeling left out. They can simply go to a pair and ask 'May I join you?' It is perfectly fine to do this activity in a group of three.

Remember to blow the whistle after every two minutes and to shout 'Change partner'. Once you see the energy flagging, perhaps after 6–10 rounds, blow the whistle twice and end the exercise.

At this point I normally ask the following questions:

- How many people met someone they thought they would like to stay in contact with? Raise your hands.

- How many people met someone and/or learned something that could help them do their job (or assist their business) more effectively? Raise your hands.

I am always surprised by the number of hands that go up and the number of new connections that are made even between people in the same organisation that could have benefited from collaboration but did not know each other or how they could assist each other before this simple yet powerful exercise.

I normally end the exercise by thanking the group who then informally mingle for the rest of the time but now know many more people than when they first came!

Something extraordinary

- **Purpose**: To generate a deeper intimacy and knowledge of participants among each other in the group. The exercise is also a good icebreaker.

- **Number of people**: 10+.

- **Equipment**: A clear space to move freely.

How to run it

This activity is contributed by speaker, broadcaster and founder of Magnificent Minds, David McQueen (**http://www. magnificent-minds.com**). Similar to the speed networking activity, this one is designed to increase intimacy in a group through a safe level of self-disclosure.

Each person is to find someone in the room and to share the answer to the three questions below:

1 What is something that they like?

2 What is something that they dislike?

3 What is something extraordinary or special about them or that they have done/experienced that not many people know about?

I have had many interesting stories in response to the last question, ranging from people being asked by Sting to dance on stage at his concert to people being invited to be a spy!

Once each couple have both shared they should then separate and both move on to find new partners. It's important to keep an eye on the group to ensure people keep moving and that the energy remains high.

People Bingo

- **Purpose**: A great icebreaker, involving disclosure, contact with others, and raising energy in a room.
- **Number of people**: 12+.
- **Equipment**: A People Bingo card. A clear space where people can move easily. Pen/pencils.

How to run it

This is one of my favourite activities which I have run in large groups of even up to 100 people. To make it work you need to prepare a 'People Bingo' card on a sheet of paper for every person and supply a pen/pencil for everyone.

A People Bingo card is simply a 4 × 3 grid with a description in each box of an experience or skill. For example:

Can speak more than three languages	Can touch their nose with the tip of their tongue	Can recite all the verses of the British National Anthem	Has seen the same musical more than three times
Who has met a member of the Royal Family	Who can play the piano	Who has won a karaoke competition	Who has had their work published
Who has been to at least two countries in Africa	Who can tell a good clean joke	Whose favourite colour is purple	Who has read *Brilliant networking*

The object is for each person to find someone in the room who has had the experience or has that particular skill. They then need to ask that person to sign their name in the relevant box on the People Bingo card to confirm that they have the experience or skill. The rule is that each box must be signed by a different person and those who claim they have the skill need to demonstrate it (where practical) before they sign their name!

The first person to complete all the boxes shouts 'Bingo' and a prize can be given. I often then read out some of the boxes from the winning card: 'Who signed that they met someone from the Royal Family? Daniel, who did you meet?'; or 'Patricia, which musical have you seen more than three times?' It helps the group to know each other better and feel more connected.

Give a time frame for the activity, for example ten minutes, to keep up the momentum. If no one has completed the activity in ten minutes, count down to discover the winner/s, for example 'Who completed 11, 10, 9, etc.?'

brilliant tip

Customise the cards with activities to suit your group. If it is within an organisation you could put something like 'find someone who has worked in more than three departments in XYZ corp' or 'find someone who started in this company via the graduate programme'. You can also customise the People Bingo cards with clip art for the items so that they look more fun and attractive. Lastly, if you have the time and access to the information, you can create a People Bingo card about an extraordinary personal fact or skill you know each individual has who is attending, or for the speakers at an event! Experiment, it's a lot of fun.

Paying it forward

This activity is suggested by Katie Ledger, a recovering TV journalist turned communications consultant and author of *And what do you do? 10 steps to creating a portfolio career* (**www.portfolio careers.net**).

- **Purpose**: To help people to move forward either personally or professionally.
- **Number of people**: 10+.
- **Equipment**: Space to move.

How to run it

Explain to all that this is an exercise in trying to help each other move forward. The idea is to get people to pair off or form groups of three whereby one person very quickly describes what they do and an area they are getting stuck on. For example, you may be setting up a business and have no experience of how to sort out the admin and financial side. The other person(s) can then advise as to how they did it (if they have had the same experience) or can suggest people/tools/websites that can help. The key is to not spend too long on each person – around three minutes maximum each. Aim to get everyone speaking to 4–8 people.

brilliant tip

If you really cannot suggest any people/tools/websites specific to that person's dilemma, just say so but be ready to pass on a general favourite of yours and say why. For example, you might suggest TED. com and comment on your favourite speaker and why. Passing on your energy and passion is positively contagious.

Different formats

Andy Lopata, who is one of the UK's leading experts on business networking strategy and who was formerly Managing Director of UK-wide network Business Referral Exchange (BRX), believes that different formats for networking events are essential (see **www.lopata.co.uk**). 'If you follow the same format for every meeting,' Andy told me, 'people start to know what they will be missing if they don't turn up. If everyone starts going through the motions and they show less enthusiasm, the network loses valuable momentum and everyone gets less value.'

Andy shared with me some of the variations of the format used in meetings while he was still involved with BRX.

Networking snowball fight

Andy said: 'I first saw this employed by a group in Croydon run by Jackie Barrie (**www.comms-plus.co.uk**), who is the Queen of trying different activities in networking groups. I always found her events to be creative and imaginative, and fun. Jackie certainly knows how to break the ice in a group.'

This event is a real icebreaker and was first used by Jackie at a Christmas networking event. Andy has since employed a variation of it in in-house training, with interesting results.

- **Purpose**: To find out how much you know about the other people in your network, or your work colleagues. To break the ice and relax everyone. To inject some fun into networking.
- **Number of people**: 10–20.
- **Equipment**: Paper and pens.

How to run it

Ask everyone to write down an unusual fact about themselves on a piece of paper. Something that, ideally, no-one else in the room will know. They should then screw the paper up into a ball.

When everyone is ready, let pandemonium ensue! Ask everyone to have a snowball fight, throwing the screwed up paper around the room: 30 seconds to a minute should be more than enough time.

When you stop everyone, ask them to pick up the nearest piece of paper to them and unravel it. Making sure they haven't got their own, ask everyone in turn to read out what is on the paper. Everyone then has to guess who wrote down each fact.

Andy told me, 'When I first ran this session one of the male group members unravelled the paper to read out "I'm pregnant"! Once the identity of the person who had written this was revealed, there was even more shock. Even her business partner didn't know!'

Some quieter members may struggle to find something they consider interesting about themselves to write down and may need a bit of gentle encouragement.

Business card swap

'This was one of the most popular exercises we used to run,' said Andy. 'In our normal meetings every member would do a 60-second presentation on their business. Every now and then we would spring this onto the unsuspecting members and find out just how much they had been taking in.'

- **Purpose**: To find out how much members of a networking group know about each other's businesses, and for individual members to find out how well they have been getting their message across.
- **Number of people**: 8–40.
- **Equipment**: Champagne bucket, top hat or similar vessel.

How to run it

On arrival ask everyone to put their business card into the champagne bucket. Before you are due to invite everyone to present their business, pass the bucket around and ask each person to draw out a card – other than their own!

Every member should then present the business of the person whose card they have drawn.

> **brilliant** tip
>
> If you know people spend time preparing their presentation, give them some kind of advance warning. Even if you don't tell them exactly what you are planning, let them know they shouldn't plan anything too specific.

Groups of three

'This takes the previous exercise a step further and really finds out how well you know each other's businesses,' said Andy. 'As for how well you get your message across, having to listen to two people get it completely wrong and not being able to say anything really brings it home.'

- **Purpose**: To find out how much members of a networking group know about each other's businesses, and for individual members to find out how well they have been getting their message across.
- **Number of people**: 3+.
- **Equipment**: Chairs in groups of three.

How to run it

Group people in threes. Pick one of the three to be in the 'spotlight'. For ten minutes the other two members then discuss that person's business, explaining in as much detail as possible to each other what their colleague does, who for and how. The person in the spotlight can only sit and listen. For ten minutes they can't say anything.

The person in the spotlight then has five minutes to respond, explaining to the other two what they said that was accurate and correcting any misunderstandings.

Over a 45-minute session you can then move the spotlight around the three members.

Try to group people with others they know fairly well. Keep visitors together and adapt the exercise so that they discuss what they *perceive* each other's businesses to involve.

What's your challenge?

'Networking should be about so much more than just collecting business cards,' Andy told me. 'Some of the most powerful results from networking come from bringing together the diverse experience, expertise and ideas of people from a range of backgrounds to help each other.' He continues, 'This exercise draws on the power of mastermind and peer-support groups and can provide some quick wins in a short period of time. The added advantage is the trust and rapport developed by seeing people really use their minds to overcome challenges.'

- **Purpose**: Helping members of a network find new approaches to overcome individual challenges. This exercise is also designed to move people away from a sales mentality and into one of helping each other.

- **Number of people**: 5–8 in each breakout would be ideal. Unlimited number of breakouts.

How to run it

Break the groups into smaller groups of around 5–8 people. In each small group ask someone who has a current business challenge to volunteer.

The volunteer has five minutes to outline the challenge to the group around them. The group then asks questions for 10–15 minutes, before being asked in turn to suggest a solution. No solutions should be provided during the questioning session.

The volunteer, who has to remain silent while the solutions are presented, then has five minutes to reply.

You can adapt the timings depending on the agenda of the meeting. I would suggest the times above are a minimum though to get any value from the activity.

brilliant tip

While you can allow a 'free for all' during the questioning session, it is advisable to put some structure to it, such as inviting each group member to ask one question first, before opening it up. This allows the quieter members of the group to contribute.

What next?!

This activity is a variation of **Paying it forward** but can be adapted to focus on any area the group wants to focus on.

- **Purpose**: To finish a networking session by firing up the group to go out and continue networking. It is about planning your next networking move by tapping into other people's networks.
- **Number of people**: 3+.
- **Equipment**: Chairs in groups of three.

How to run it

Group people in threes. Pick one of the three to be in the 'spot-light'. This person needs to identify an area that they need to improve on. For three minutes the other two members then discuss people they know who could help, or provide ideas of books, sources they could use, etc. The person in the spotlight can only sit and listen. After three minutes the group moves on to the next person. The aim is to keep the rhythm and energy flowing – remember this is an exercise to close the session, so be strict with the three minutes! You can increase the group size as this means you get more quality contributions but you need to then decrease the time for each participant.

'It is great to see people swapping numbers or scribbling references onto their notebooks as they exchange information. I think that is how any networking session should finish,' says Elena Moreno, who regularly uses this closing exercise for sessions with undergraduates and postgraduates who are developing and stretching their networking skills. 'I find that it is important to encourage the group to really take their networking outside the specific session I've just delivered.' Elena is an educator, facilitator and trainer who works at the University of Greenwich. She has a great blog on careers at **www. Careercallings.blogspot.com**.

☀ brilliant tip

This exercise can be turned into an inspiring handout that you distribute to participants as they leave the networking event. It could have the format of Top Ten Tips of things they could action in the next week, encouraging them to expand their networks.
The ultimate purpose of **What next?!** is to encourage participants to continue networking and to put their networking skills to use.

Personal treasure

This process is contributed by David Pearl, founder of the personal and professional development company Pearl Group (**www.pearlgroup.net**) and the Realise programme, and is based on the 'Personal Still Life' process developed by Liz and Charles Handy (**www.lizhandy.net**). David Pearl is a creative consultant to some of the world's leading businesses which use 'Experience Engineering' to make work and life more inspired and inspiring.

- **Purpose**: To allow a group quickly to connect and share their values in an enjoyable and non-intellectual way; to get beyond the business card stuffiness and into the richness of conversation. It works well both with complete strangers and with groups that want to know each other at a deeper level.
- **Number of people**: Can work with any group size.
- **Equipment**: Personal objects brought by participants.

How to run it

Each person is asked to bring to the meeting two objects, each of which will easily fit into their pocket. One represents 'something I care deeply about', the other 'what I am proudest of in my working life'.

Just considering this question is valuable for attendees and means that your event begins to be intriguing days or weeks in advance.

The great thing about objects is they are often easier to talk about than ourselves (especially to strangers). And yet the value we place on these small things says far more about us than our small talk or CV-chat.

It is important to point out that the objects do not need to be valuable in themselves – in fact they probably should not be – but they represent important aspects of life for the delegate.

There are many ways of using these objects to help people network:

1　Smaller groups can sit together (with wine!) and each person in turn places their objects on the table and takes a couple of minutes to explain their significance. It is helpful to place the objects on a piece of A4 paper to 'frame' them like a piece of art, which helps them to be seen properly.

2　Larger groups can mingle in a room, spending a few minutes with a partner showing and explaining the objects and then moving on (a bit like the speed dating exercise earlier).

3　You can set up an object gallery. Delegates arrive and place their objects on pieces of paper in an empty room. Later, when the networking moment is required, the delegates wander the room, like art lovers, trying to guess which objects belong to which delegates. This adds a nice puzzle solving element to the process. It also helps people examine their preconceptions of other people.

brilliant tip

You can do this exercise with just one object, but it's nicer to have a couple so you can ask delegates to look out for connections between the two objects. Some people have a close match between what they care about and what they do. In other cases the connection is not so clear and it can be helpful for one delegate to ask another: 'I am curious about the connection between these two objects for you: will you explain?' We have had letters months after from people who have realised that their work has very little to do with what they really care about and have set about changing their jobs! Not bad for a quick and entertaining networking exercise.

Conversational canape

This is a variation of the above activity which requires no preparation on the part of the delegates and can be an excellent alternative if you cannot communicate with people in advance.

- **Purpose**: To facilitate connection and deepen the conversation between people who do not know each other well in a low key, social setting. It works particularly well to inject some intrigue and fun into an otherwise formal cocktail party.
- **Number of people**: Limited only by the objects you find (see below). We have done this with small groups of 15–30, but it can also work with 100+ provided you are prepared to set it up.
- **Equipment**: Catering trays (and staff). Objects.

How to run it

This activity is based on **Personal treasure** (earlier) and is a technique also used in the Pearl Group's personal reinvention programme Realise.

In advance of your event you find or buy a collection of completely different small objects, small enough to fit at least ten on a tray. You will need at least one for every guest. They can be anything – a pen, a shell, a coin, a nail, a key, a stamp, a clothes peg, old watch, kid's toy, fork, egg cup, screwdriver and so on. Old or used stuff is often best.

Your guests find themselves in a normal cocktail party setting except that (at an agreed moment) the caterers walk round with trays filled with these intriguing objects. (If the event is not catered, you can simply leave the objects on a tray or table as they enter. But do make sure someone is inviting the guests to choose one or they may be overlooked.) The guests are asked to choose one object and once they have they need to tell their fellow guests why they chose that object. Who or what does it remind them of? How does it connect with what is valuable and important in their lives? It is a surprising and fun way to get below the skin and tell stories from the past that you wouldn't normally share except with friends and family.

Guests will often ask if they can keep the objects and we recommend that they are treated as gifts.

Another way to frame this question is to ask (either verbally or using a sign on the tray): 'Which object chooses you?' You are encouraging people really to look and then sense which object 'jumps out' at them. It is amazing how often people will pick an object and say, with wonder, *how did you know this was so important to me?*

brilliant tip

You can enrich the networking experience for your guests by giving some time and attention to the objects you select in advance. Yes, you can simply toddle off to the supermarket with a shopping list. But it can be more effective – and magical – if you spend a few days just thinking about the people who will come (as you would at a small dinner party). While you keep these people in mind – and the experience you want for them – just keep your eyes open for objects that seem to fit. You will be amazed how many objects are just lying around waiting to be picked up. Second-hand objects that have been owned and used are particularly powerful so check your junk and charity shops. And if you are near a beach, stones and shells are perfect – they seem to bring out strong memories for people! We find doing this advance work heightens the connection that participants make with the random objects and makes the exercise itself even more potent.

Summary

Networking does not always happen by accident and some care in designing the right conditions or activities for people to share and meet others can really deepen connections. I hope you will try out some of these activities and also hope you will share your experiences or effective activities with me.

If you have any activities that you think other readers can benefit from do e-mail me at *steven@brilliantnetworking.net* and if I include your activity in a new edition I will mention your name alongside it! So, get networking!

Conclusion

Hopefully by now, when someone mentions the word 'networking' you don't cringe. You know that it is much more than a simple exchange of business cards and, most importantly, you have the confidence and skills you need to network brilliantly in *all* areas of your life.

Remember, many brilliant networkers developed their skills through practice, sometimes making many mistakes, collecting lots of rejections, but eventually achieving their goals and assisting others to achieve theirs. The key is to apply what you have learnt in this book to your work, your relationships – anywhere you can connect with others. When you do connect effortlessly you'll know it is time to pass on this book to someone else to help them become a brilliant networker too.

Brilliant networkers don't really say 'goodbye' for good because they know their paths might cross again. My wish for you is that you use the networking skills in this book to create the life you want and that you connect with me and the brilliant networking community to share your success with others.

Happy networking!

Steven D'Souza
www.brilliantnetworking.net

Appendix

This section contains a range of resources, links to websites and networking groups to get your journey as a brilliant networker going.

Brilliant networking community

Please visit our website **www.brilliantnetworking.net** where you will have access to lots of free 'stuff', including articles on networking and presentations, details of how to book me as a speaker and the 'Brilliant Networking' training course. You will find links to a wide range of networks, people and groups you can connect with to assist in achieving your goals. Since the launch of *Brilliant networking* I have done dozens of dynamic keynote talks and interactive workshops for groups large and small, for business networks, charities and global firms. I would be happy to explore speaking to your group or company.

Please also feel free to contact me, Steven D'Souza, at **Steven@brilliantnetworking.net**, with your thoughts on the book, your tips, stories and questions. I'd be delighted to hear from you.

Useful books

How to Develop a Perfect Memory (1994) by Dominic O'Brien, Headline.

Four times world memory champion, Dominic O'Brien shares dozens of tips to remember names, faces, dates and other useful information for networking.

Achieving Success through Social Capital (2000) by Wayne Baker, John Wiley & Sons.

This is the best book I have read on social capital and how to develop your own social capital. There is a quiz inside and lists of tips to develop your network in an organisational setting or as an entrepreneur.

You're Great – Three Steps to Self-Confidence (1995) by Julia Hastings, Touchstone Publications.

This book highlights the tool of mental picturing to unlock self-confidence.

Shortcuts to Bliss (1998) by Jonathan Robinson, Conari Press.

A practical guide of 50 tips to improve your relationships and connect to your dreams.

The Power of Networking (1999) by Sandy Villas and Donna Fisher, Thorsons.

Written by coaches and network club founders, this book is crammed with techniques and tools for networking.

Personal Networking (2003) by Nick Cope, FT Prentice Hall.

This is a brilliant book on using networking to maximise social capital. Lots of useful models to help grow and maintain your network.

The Ultimate Guide to Successful Networking (2004) by Carole Stone, Vermilion.

A practical book containing dozens of tips for effective networking and hosting your own networking events.

Bridging the Culture Gap (2004) by Penny Carte and Chris Fox, Kogan Page.

A practical guide to the different dimensions of international business communication.

The Networking Survival Guide (2003) by Diane Darling, McGraw-Hill.

A practical guide to networking with a range of websites listed in the resource section.

And Death Came Third (2006) by Andy Lopata, Lean Marketing Press.

A book on successful presenting, networking and public speaking.

Brilliant Presentations (2006) by Richard Hall, Prentice Hall.

General networking link

http://en.wikipedia.org/wiki/List_of_social_networking_websites

Brilliant links

1   www.mindjet.com

2   www.thebrain.com

3   www.studentvoice.co.uk

Business networking organisations

Business Link: www.businesslink.gov.uk

Contains valuable information on starting and growing your business, and a search engine for a list of business events in your area.

BNI: www.bni-europe.com

An established business referral organisation with chapters across the globe.

Chambers of Commerce online: www.chamberonline.co.uk
The British Chambers of Commerce have a wide geographical spread with more than 56 local Chambers of Commerce in the UK and a network of Chambers across the globe.

Federation of Small Businesses: www.fsb.org.uk
Formed in 1974, it now has over 205,000 members across 33 regions and 230 branches. Aimed at small businesses and the self-employed, it runs a variety of regular events.

Intelligent Networking Events: www.getnetworking.co.uk
Started by the entrepreneur Pat Philpott, this website contains links to events for local businesses.

For entrepreneurs

Make your Mark: www.starttalkingideas.org
This website has a link to dozens of connectors who have started their own networks and businesses deriving from networking. This is the best site I have seen, bringing together a range of networkers.

Connection sites

LinkedIn: www.linkedin.com
A site for career networking with over 11 million users. Free and easy to set up. Other related sites that are useful to explore are:

www.rickupton.com/linkedin-tips.htm

www.askdavetaylor.com/how_do_i_use_linkedin_to_find_a_job.html

http://blog.guykawasaki.com/2007/01/ten_ways_to_use.html

www.thevirtualhandshake.com/blog/2005/11/09/ten-ways-to-use-linkedin-to-build-your-business

www.thisisgoingtobebig.com/2005/05/not_the_way_to_.html

www.linkedintelligence.com/smart-ways-to-use-linkedin

www.thinkinghomebusiness.com/blog/_archives/
2007/4/6/2862064.html

Facebook: www.facebook.com

A free site allowing you to upload photos, network
confidentially with friends, post videos and join networks.

Bebo: www.bebo.com

Bebo is an online community allowing you to share photos and
blogs. Others have the facility to draw on a 'whiteboard' on
your site. You have complete control over who is invited into
your list and confidentiality is maintained.

Horse's Mouth: www.horsesmouth.co.uk

The first informal e-mentoring site allowing you to connect
with others to give and share advice as a mentor or mentee.

Wikis

www.wikihow.com/Start-a-Wiki

A useful guide on how to start your own wiki.

Wiki sites on social networking:

http://en.wikipedia.org/wiki/List_of_social_networking_
websites

www.ning.com

www.writenews.com/2004/060404_social_networking.htm

http://en.wikinews.org/wiki/Bloggers_investigate_social_
networking_websites

Blogs

Gerald West: http://bobowest.blogspot.com

Here there are brilliant articles on the concept of Flow, CSD
and other personal development articles.

The Daily Networker: www.dailynetworker.co.uk
Run by Oli Barrett, this contains useful information relating to networking and links to other networking blogs.

Connecting People: http://networkingandreferrals. blogspot.com
Blog by Andy Lopata, former Managing Director of the Business Referral Exchange.

Damien Senn: www.senn-sational.com
Internet business coaching and website of the founder of Web Wednesdays.

Andy Lopata: www. lopata.co.uk
Former MD of the Business Referral Exchange, Andy speaks frequently about networking.

YouGovStone: www.yougovstone.com
A partnership between YouGov market research agency and the networking expert Carole Stone, this organisation brings together opinion formers on a range of important public policy subjects.

Guides on how to start a blog

www.maximumawesome.com/bloggingtips.htm

www.blogger.com

www.bbc.co.uk/webwise/askbruce/articles/browse/ makeblog_1.shtml

http://office.microsoft.com/en-us/help/ HA101726561033. aspx

www.blogcatalog.com/blogs/a-step-by-step-guide-to-create-dynamic-blog.html

Forums

UK Business Forums: www.ukbusinessforums.co.uk
A connection of different business forums allowing you to share your views on franchising to e-commerce.

Contact management

Plaxo: www.plaxo.com
For those with Microsoft Outlook, Plaxo lets you automatically synchronise your address book, even across multiple computers. Outlook users can also synchronise their calendar, tasks and notes to access them anywhere on Plaxo Online.

Microsoft Outlook: www.outlookpower.com/issues/ issue200207/contact001.html
A guide to using one of the world's most common and accessible office/work tools.

Coaches

Brad Meyer: www.collaboration.co.uk
Brad is a leading expert in using technology and multimedia to assist teams and groups to collaborate effectively.

NLP and communication skills

NLP was developed by Richard Bandler and John Grinder in 1960s' California. It has now become an international field of study in how to model excellence and is adopted by trainers around the world.

NLP Academy: www.nlpacademy.co.uk
Provides a range of learning tools, including monthly groups and certification training with leading experts in NLP.

Public speaking

The National Association of Toastmasters: www.natuk.com
The association runs courses throughout the UK in public
speaking skills.

Volunteering websites

Timebank: www.timebank.org.uk
Provides information on volunteering charities both in the UK
and abroad.

Social network analysis tools

There is a range of effective social network analysis tools provided by Humax Corporation. Visit **www.humaxnetworks.
com** for more information.

The three tools that I recommend are:

● *Humax Assessment of Social Capital*
  Who's in your core network? How are they connected? And
  what does all this tell you about the strength of your social
  capital? Where do you need to build and invest? Take the
  online Humax Assessment for an accurate – and revealing –
  picture of your social network, profile type and diagnostics.
  Once you've completed the assessment you instantly get
  your customised analysis online.

brilliant tip

Readers of *Brilliant networking* get a special discount:
visit www.humaxnetworks.com/contactus.asp and enter 'Humax
Assessment discount preapproved for Brilliant Networkers' in the
Enter Your Questions or Comments here field.

- *Organisational assessment*
  Humax's online organisational assessment produces maps of energising and de-energising connections in your organisation, identifying the bright stars who energise others and the black holes who suck energy out of the system. With these energy maps, you can locate and replicate the positive practices that create energy. In addition, you can identify and fix the negative practices that drain energy.

- *Reciprocity Ring*™
  The Reciprocity Ring™ is an energising exercise that enables the principle of pass it forward in your group. Engage in a Reciprocity Ring™ and you'll witness in real time the potential of social networking. During your Reciprocity Ring™ experiences you:
  - learn the power and practice of reciprocity
  - find solutions to your issues while focusing on contributions to others
  - build trust as you learn about and help one another.

For more on social network analysis and a range of conferences and events visit International Network for Social Network Analysis at **www.insna.org**

the brilliant series

Fast and engaging, the *Brilliant* series works hard to make sure you stand out from the crowd. Each *Brilliant* book has been carefully crafted to ensure everything you read is practical and applicable – to help you make a difference now.

9780273722328

9780273720591

9780273717355

9780273743217

9780273726463

9780273725114

9780273721239

9780273712350

9780273734147

9780273714804

9780273730675

9780273730910

9780273720799 · **brilliant Business Writing** · How to inspire, engage and persuade through words

9780273727347 · **brilliant Copywriting** · How to craft the most interesting and effective copy imaginable

9780273721826 · **brilliant Meetings** · What to know, do and say to have fewer, better meetings

9780273738077 · **brilliant Customer Service** · What to know, do and say to keep your customers happy

9780273737452 · **brilliant Online Marketing** · What to know and do to successfully market your business online

9780273742555 · **brilliant Email Productivity** · How to win back time and take control of your inbox

9780273744092 · **brilliant Time Management** · What the most productive people know, do and say

9780273724902 · **brilliant Cognitive Behavioural Therapy**

9780273732556 · **brilliant NLP** · What the most successful people know, do and say

9780273740544 · **brilliant Influence** · What the most influential people know, do and say

9780273735885 · **brilliant Confidence** · How to challenge your fears and go for anything you want in life

9780273723271 · **brilliant Retirement** · Everything you need to know and do to make the most of your golden years

Whatever your level, we'll get you to the next one. It's all about you. Get ready to shine!

Prentice Hall
is an imprint of